Fear of Death
It's About Life, Actually

Let's Talk About It

Amy Wallace, M.A.

Cover Design: Fishman Design
Truro, Massachusetts
www.fishmandesign.com
Photo by the author

to
My Parents

with
Love and Gratitude

Table of Contents

For what is it to die but to stand
naked in the wind and to melt into the
sun?
And what is it to cease breathing, but
to free the breath from its restless tides,
that it may rise and expand and seek God
unencumbered?

Only when you drink from the river of
silence shall you indeed sing.
And when you have reached the
mountain top, then you shall begin to
climb.
And when the earth shall claim your
limbs, then shall you truly dance.

From "On Death" in <u>The Prophet</u> by Kahlil Gibran

Preface

This inquiry or conversation is an opportunity for all of us to look deeply at our attitudes, fears, blind-spots, possibilities, and hopes about death. It could change – for the better – how we live our lives *and* our deaths.

There is a natural kind of progression to this book, so I think it will be useful (although certainly not required) to go through the book in order. We start where many of us are about death – in Fear and Denial; the first chapter looks at what keeps so many of us from looking into or engaging with death (until we are forced to), as well as the costs to our aliveness resulting from not inquiring into the fact and reality of our mortality.

The second chapter asks what might be possible when we do take a look at death – how it might affect the lives we lead, as well as the deaths we experience. There are questions we can ask ourselves in order to deepen the inquiry . . . sometimes just asking them is a way of giving ourselves more power in our relationship to death.

The third chapter offers 5 practices – useful for living more consciously and happily on a daily basis, to be sure – but also helpful when we imagine facing death, as well as when the time comes for us to actually die.

I recommend taking the time and space to experience the chapter "Imagining Death – an Ancient Practice", and write down everything that comes up – it's all good information, from the most reliable source about you – *you*! There will be ideas, tools, and practices for working with all of it in the subsequent chapters, so letting all the "material" surface will help produce the most value. The final chapters are intended to leave us feeling more at home with the idea of dying, and more empowered to live fully.

Appendix A is a list of books and other resources that I have encountered and appreciated in my own inquiries about death and life. Many of the authors listed are well known and esteemed for their work in the field of death and dying; the list can be a useful wealth of resources for your own inquiry.

Appendix B contains some additional quotes and writings for further contemplation.

The new century has already given us many changes and challenges; we have much opportunity – and probably necessity – to open ourselves to one another and share the journey. Let's talk . . . about death, life, what scares or inspires us, where we need help and what help we can offer.

We're all just walking each other home.
Ram Dass

Amy Wallace, M.A. Counseling Psychology
Santa Cruz Mountains, California, USA
April 2013

Introduction

*It all boils down to the fear of death,
arguably the cause of most of our
unhappiness. We unknowingly harm our
loved ones out of fear; we hold ourselves
back personally and professionally for the
same reason. Since every fear has its
roots in the fear of death, learning to relax
about the fear surrounding death will
allow us to face everything else with
greater ease.*
Elisabeth Kübler-Ross and David Kessler, <u>Life Lessons</u>

"Let's talk about death."   Not exactly a great
conversation starter. You can usually get people to
agree that we don't talk about it, but that's as far as it
goes. I was once in a room full of therapists – new
friends, all great people – and I started to talk about
this book I wanted to write about facing death. Yes,
everyone agreed, we don't talk about death in our
culture. So I asked a couple of questions about why
they thought we didn't, and what if we did, and
someone cleverly said "could we change the subject,
please?" It took me a few seconds to realize they
weren't joking! They really didn't want to talk about it.
And these were therapists – some of the very people
you expect to be able to help you when you're ready to
deal with death.

I wrote this book for all of us . . . given that every one of us will die, I've noticed that any conversation about death is *conspicuously missing* from our lives. I believe we need to talk about death, look deeply within ourselves about it, examine our beliefs about it and come to a place of acceptance – true acceptance, not just resignation.

Most of us know of someone whose final moments, days, or longer, were spent in agony which could, perhaps, have been avoided if the person and their loved ones had talked about death in advance. Well-meaning medical professionals sometimes cause a dying person more pain trying to keep them alive at all costs – again, because the person's wishes weren't made known in advance, or because their family wasn't ready to let them go.

Things are changing . . . Hospice is now widely available to those with a terminal diagnosis who would like to spend their last moments at home, with their family and friends and with others who are trained to help them die with dignity and some measure of peace. People can make their wishes known about how they would and would not like to spend their last moments in this life . . . provided they have been willing to face the reality that they will die and to make and communicate these choices in advance.

Death should not be dealt with only once we are in the hospital or on our deathbed . . . it is a part of life and a most important one. Each of us deserves to have absolutely the best possible death experience we can have – the commitment to which clearly also enhances our experience of living, increases our awareness of the impact of our actions, and helps motivate us to create true meaning in our lives.

Let's talk about it! Let's have conversations about the reality of our mortality, our fears about death *and* life; learn about others' experiences around death, and about what we can do for ourselves and people we care about.

As Ram Dass says in the videotaped workshop "Dying Into Love" . . .

Dying is the most important ceremony in life.

The fact that each of us will die is one of the very few things we can count on in this life. Perhaps we can allow that fact to empower us to live more consciously, with more aliveness, satisfaction, gratitude, meaning, and purpose . . . and to die more consciously – with more aliveness, satisfaction, and gratitude – as we graduate from this school of life into whatever comes next.

Why Don't We Talk About Death?

*One of the chief reasons we have so much
anguish and difficulty facing death is that
we ignore the truth of impermanence. We
so desperately want everything to continue
as it is that we have to believe that things
will always stay the same. But this is only
make-believe.*
Sogyal Rinpoche, *The Tibetan Book of Living and Dying*

Here are some of the answers I hear when I ask people
why they don't talk about death:

- **Denial**: I don't want to think about it; I'll think
  about it later; there's plenty of time for that;
  other people don't want to talk about it; it's
  morbid, impolite, depressing, inappropriate.

- **Dissatisfaction**: I'm not that happy with how
  my life is; it'll be better in the future, when (fill
  in the blank) happens; I'm not ready; I haven't
  really lived yet.

- **Fear of . . .** pain, change, the unknown, losing
  faculties, losing control, leaving loved ones,

unfinished business, not having lived a meaningful life, what comes after.

- **Resignation** (sometimes disguised as acceptance): There's nothing I can do about it, so why talk about it?; it's just a fact of life; it happens to all of us.

- **Superstition**: If I talk about it, it might happen sooner.

I believe that – looking closely – we see that it pretty much all comes down to *fear*. But I do believe it's important to examine the variety of reasons we give ourselves, since fear is often hidden inside resignation, procrastination, denial, or whatever our particular form of not-looking-at-death might be.

So, let's take a closer look . . .

Denial

Many of us live our lives as if we had all the time in the world. And what does that cost us?

Man . . . sacrifices his health in order to make money. Then he sacrifices money to recuperate his health. And then he is so anxious about the future that he does not enjoy the present; the result being that he does not live in the present or the future;

11

he lives as if he is never going to die, and
then dies having never really lived.
from an interview with His Holiness The Dalai
Lama

Have you ever come away from a funeral service feeling the urgency of life? The unpredictability of death? Especially if the person who died was really close to you and even more especially if they were very young? Did you vow to stop procrastinating? To appreciate life more? To let people know more often that you love them? To make that phone call you'd been putting off, or to find the courage to do or be what you really wanted?

How long did that sense of urgency last? Why did it fade away?

We live inside a culture of denial of death – it's not just a personal foible that has us tend to ignore it. So even when we decide to be more present for life, to stop procrastinating, to be aware that we could die at any moment – just like the person whose funeral we just attended – there is an almost irresistible pull back into denial, back into a kind of sleep or amnesia about the reality of death.

Many people receive a diagnosis of terminal illness. Some choose to use this "advance notice" as an opportunity to clean up any unfinished business, to come to terms with their lives and deaths. Others choose to "fight" to the very end, maybe even refusing to deal with the practical issues that would help their loved ones during and after their death.

12

Certainly the mainstream medical profession will keep someone alive as long as they can, unless directed otherwise by the dying person or their family. Is death the enemy – to be feared, vilified, denied, and avoided at all costs? Is dying a kind of failure?

The thing is, death is always there – whether in the forefront of our awareness, in the background, or submerged under the things we occupy our minds with so we don't think about it. It's one of the "bookends" – birth and death – that bracket what we call our life. Or, as many cultures believe, it's one transition point in the endless cycle of life – the ending of something as well as the beginning of something else.

One of my good friends is a beautiful woman I've known since she was 29 years old. On her 30th birthday, she was sad that she was no longer 21; there was such a bittersweet feeling in that celebration. On her 40th birthday, she wished she were 30, and on her 50th birthday, she longed to be 40 again. She acknowledges how much she has missed by being stuck in and romanticizing the past (the very past in which she didn't appreciate being younger and more beautiful at the time), and that there is an underlying *fear* – that each birthday brings her closer to "the end".

Why would any of us be afraid or sad about being closer to the end? In addition to our concerns about the dying process and leaving loved ones, might we regret the time spent either in the past or in the future, not really being present for the moments of beauty and love that we do have?

And this begs the questions, why *don't* we live present to the amazing possibilities of every moment? What keeps us from knowing and being who we really are or doing what we really want? And how could it be different, both during our life and at the time of our death?

Perhaps we have a fundamental misunderstanding about our true nature, our own divinity, our own power to create and live lives that we love. We tend to see ourselves as *separate* – from others, from Nature, from the ultimate creative force of the universe (sometimes known as "God") – and many believe that experience of separate-ness is the basis of most of our problems and our unhappiness, as individuals and in our relationships with all other living beings, including our beloved Mother, Earth. Might this be one of the most important inquiries of all?

Fear

One of the most universal and profound fears of all is the fear of dying without having really lived, dying unfulfilled. This is the fear that underlies many of the other forms of fear: that we will die without having found or created meaning in our lives; that we will wait too long to take the risks, express ourselves, love fully, stop caring so much about what other people think; or that we'll fail to identify and acknowledge what's really important to us and go after it.

The irony is that it's also fear that keeps us from taking the risks and making the changes we need to make in order to create that sense of fulfillment for ourselves. How do we interrupt that vicious cycle?

The key is in understanding to what extent and in what areas fear controls us. You may have heard people say that FEAR is an acronym: *False **E**vidence **A**ppearing **R**eal*. This way of thinking of fear helps me remember that – except when there actually *is* a lion chasing me – when fear comes up, it doesn't necessarily mean I should abandon what I'm doing or

15

dreaming of doing. There may be some useful information for me in the fear – especially if I'm observing the fear rather than being controlled by it – but I shouldn't automatically let it keep me from living my life.

Here is the true purpose of this book: learning to use the awareness of our own mortality to encourage and inspire us (or kick us lovingly in the butt) through the fears and other limitations that keep us from living as fully and fulfilled as possible.

So – before we look at what we fear about *death*, let's look at what scares us in *life* . . .

Dying is easy, it's living that scares me to death.
Annie Lennox, "Cold"

Consider Thich Nhat Hanh's quote at the beginning of this section: what does he mean when he says "We are filled with the fear of annihilation"? I submit that this is true not only with regard to dying, but whenever we consider doing something that scares us. But is it actual physical annihilation we're afraid of, or is it the death of who we think we are, who we consider ourselves to be, our reputation, our bank account or whatever else we think protects or determines who we are?

What are we afraid of? We're afraid . . .

  - we won't succeed

  - we're too old (whatever that means)

16

- we're too young (ditto)

- people will say we're crazy, irresponsible, stupid, or selfish

- things could get out of control

- (insert your worst fear here)

Now think back to a time you really wanted to do something and you were afraid, but you did it anyway. Maybe it was when you decided to ask for a raise or promotion at work, to ask someone to go out with you, and you knew you'd just die if they said "no", but you did it anyway. What happened? If they said "no" – did you die? If they said "yes" – did you realize you needn't have been so afraid? *F*alse *E*vidence *A*ppearing *R*eal.

Again, Thich Nhat Hanh: "When we understand that we cannot be destroyed, we are liberated from fear." In his book he's talking specifically about the Buddhist belief that we don't really die – there's no such thing as death. But see how well it applies to all of life - all the scary potential "little deaths" we face along the way.

We see people doing things that seem really bold and courageous – taking risks in order to engage in activities that make their hearts sing, even without the "safety nets" *we* might want to have in place. Might it be that it's scarier to imagine dying unfulfilled, dying with remorse or regret, dying without knowing who they might have been? How might we use the fear of dying unfulfilled to inspire and motivate us to take risks for a life we truly love?

17

There are often times when expanding who I am means shedding the skin of who I've been or who I believe myself to be, and it can be *terrifying*. Sometimes it really feels like who I am is dying, and all the things I usually "know" and understand temporarily go out the window. In fact, I've experienced it during the writing of this book. Given that I'm writing a book about facing the fear of death, I see that it's not surprising. I am thankful for the friends I have who are also committed to consciously evolving and can remind me that what's happening to me is not The End.

Taking leaps of faith – believing that when we jump off, the path will appear under our feet – takes practice. Once we've had the experience a few times, we begin to realize that maybe this is the way we're supposed to live life and evolve ourselves. Or at least, this is one way – an exciting way – which can bring so much more to our lives than always "playing it safe".

Each of us has what could be called our "comfort zone" – smaller and tighter in some domains and more expansive and less constraining in other areas. But instead of moving freely outside of our comfort zones in order to try something new or scary, we often find ourselves staying put, as if constrained by an actual barrier. It may be quite a while before we notice that our comfort zone has become a no-growth zone and that there's really nothing holding us back other than that False Evidence Appearing Real.

Fear of the Dying Process Itself

As many of us watch our parents age, lose their faculties, and suffer with pain and frustration, we wonder if everyone has to age and die this way – will we have to go through this pain and suffering? Will we be a burden on our family? This fear is exacerbated by several aspects of our culture, among them a near-worship of youth and staying young and alive at all costs; the costs of long-term care; the dissolution of the "family unit" with children living far from their parents; the lack of choices and control over how we die; and lack of planning regarding legal matters and how we want to die (often because of denial). To the extent that we are willing to think and dialogue about these issues *before* we are dying, they can be addressed.

Many of us are afraid of the physical pain we might have to endure when we die; I know I have some fear about that. The goal of *palliative care* is to allow someone to move through the dying process as pain-free as possible. Doctors have gained much more understanding about pain management in recent decades and are often able to achieve this goal during a person's last months, weeks, and hours, even if they are dying not in a hospital, but at home or in hospice.

But pain can't always be avoided, and some people live with pain for a long time before dying.

One thing we can do is learn to take advantage of the power of the mind to influence the body, by using such

19

tools as *meditation* or *deep breathing*; these are easy to learn and can be beneficial to us throughout our lives. Becoming familiar with them "in advance", so to speak, makes it easier to call on these tools when there is pain.

Many validated studies have shown that regular meditation strengthens our immune system, lowers stress and high blood pressure, and allows us to be more calm and present in life, even when we're *not* meditating. And meditation does not have to be complicated or involve anything "weird" – it's really just breathing, focusing the mind (or de-focusing it from the everyday "noise"), noticing, and going inside yourself. You can find books about it or join a class or group to learn more.

Breathing – while a normal function we can't help doing – is not usually fully used or appreciated in everyday life. Notice right now whether you're breathing deeply or not. (I often catch myself holding my belly in, which isn't very conducive to breathing deeply.) Oxygen and fresh air aren't just necessities – when you get good amounts through deep breathing, they are actually healing. Just the shift in focus and the bodily movements required to breathe deeply can bring about a noticeable shift in your awareness and your mood. Check it out! And imagine how it could help, during the dying process (or any time you *feel* like you're dying), to be able to calm and soothe yourself with meditation and deep breathing, or to support someone else in doing so during their dying process.

20

For breathing exercises, I highly recommend two CDs, listed under Books in Appendix A; I use these exercises when I feel anxiety, fear, or pain; they're very effective and always available to us:

1. "Breathing – the Master Key to Self Healing" by Andrew Weil, M.D.

2. "Breathe to Beat the Blues" by Amy Weintraub

When there is pain, a simple prayer or meditation, like this one offered by Zen Buddhist priest Joan Halifax in <u>Being with Dying</u>, can be of help:

- May I find the inner resources to be open to my pain.

- May I turn toward my pain with kindness.

- May I observe my pain with equanimity.

- May I realize that this pain is not permanent.

- May I let go of my expectations around my pain.

- May I know that I am not my pain, not my body, not my illness.

- May I accept pain, knowing it does not make me bad or wrong.

- May I accept my pain, knowing that my heart is not limited by it.

Favorite pieces of music can help us relax and would be helpful when we're dying. If we're willing to address these things in advance and let our loved ones know what we'd like – there are many ways to make this most important part of our life the best experience it can possibly be. (Some of my favorite pieces of music are listed under "Recommended Resources" in Appendix A.)

Our emotions and attitudes about death (and life and who or what we really are) will also have a big impact on the pain we experience, which is why it's so important to engage in this inquiry before we're in the process of actually dying.

> *. . . actually, pain can be our greatest teacher, once we stop frantically fleeing its presence . . . The sensation of pain is bad enough. But it's . . . the story we tell ourselves about our pain that's the real trouble. Try saying to yourself, the next time you feel pain, "I am in pain but I am not suffering." See if it helps to remind you not to amplify the pain by building a story around it.*
> Joan Halifax, *Being with Dying*

There are two phrases in this quote I'd like to explore a little: "the story we tell ourselves" and "I am in pain but I am not suffering".

In the first phrase, Ms. Halifax is making a distinction between what is actually happening and what we tell ourselves or think to ourselves about what is happening. In this case, *pain* is what's happening; the *story* might sound something like, "I didn't think

22

there'd be this much pain, I can't handle it, why is this happening to me?, am I being punished?, I'd better not let people see I'm in pain" or any other thoughts that we add to purely experiencing the pain.

We do this all the time – it's part of being human – there is *what's so* (the facts, what's observable, that everyone could agree on), and then there's the *story*, the narrative that we add to it. And by story, I don't mean lies in the sense that we're purposely inventing something in order to deceive someone. But we do invent it – we add the story to the simple facts.

Even a simple thing such as arriving late for an appointment . . . how often do we simply say, "I'm late, I apologize"? It's more likely to sound like "I tried to get here on time, there must have been an accident, and you know my roommate just had to spend an hour in the shower this morning" . . . Notice what story you might be telling yourself right now – about anything: what are the facts, and what judgments, assessments, explanations, or excuses are you adding? What happens when you take them away and just notice what's so?

This practice of distinguishing what's so from the story is a powerful capability . . . life-transforming, really. When we get to the sections on "5 Practices for More Conscious Living and Dying" and "Mining the Gold", we'll find this practice to be very useful in helping us take ownership; be complete; be present; and let go of resentments, regrets, and unfinished business.

What do you now see about the phrase "I am in pain, but I am not suffering"? The word 'suffering' in this context has to do with the story I'm telling myself about the pain, doesn't it? "I had a misunderstanding with a good friend, but I'm not suffering." "The picnic was canceled because of rain, and I'm not suffering." "I gained two pounds over the weekend, and I'm not suffering." "I'm very sad that my father died, and I'm not suffering."

What causes suffering is resistance – the unwillingness to accept or embrace what's so. Resistance causes us to contract – physically, mentally, emotionally – which causes or increases pain and diminishes our ability to be, to respond or be *response-able*. For increasing one's ability to accept whatever is happening, I recommend any of Pema Chödrön's work, and especially <u>When Things Fall Apart</u>.

We put up resistance so often in our lives. And what are most of us resisting more than death? No wonder it is such a painful experience for so many of us.

Another aspect of how we die has to do with making our wishes known in advance about how we'd like to die, what measures we do or do not want to be taken to keep us alive, and so on. We can make these wishes known – both informally and legally – to the people who might be present when we die, and we'll address some of this in "Making Your Wishes Known – Legal and Practical Issues". But clearly - in order to take these steps – we need to face our denial and fear.

Fear of Losing Control

Believing we are in control . . . At some point – or many points – along the way, most of us discover that we are not really in control of much in life. But we seem to think we are, much of the time, and it's hard to let go of that belief until we are forced to.

The notion of surrendering or letting go is something we will explore in depth in the chapter "5 Practices for More Conscious Living and Dying". From my point of view, the ability to surrender (not giving up but letting go of resistance) is one of the most important and powerful capabilities we can develop for a satisfying life . . . and death.

Also – being able to distinguish between what we can control and what we can't gives us a lot more peace of mind (we'll look at some tools for doing this in the chapter "Mining the Gold - Working with What Comes Up"). What we *can* control, we can address and influence. What we *can't* control we can either resist, which will cause more pain, or we can embrace, accept, let go of resisting or trying to control.

Fear of Change

> *At one's core there is an ever-present conflict between the wish to continue to exist and the awareness of inevitable death.*
> Irvin D. Yalom, *Love's Executioner*

25

The fear of change is related to the fear of losing control and – really – any kind of loss. Doesn't it make sense that the way you approach change in life is likely to be the way you approach death?

Think about how you feel about change . . . Do you choose it? Embrace it? Do you have such a strong sense of who you really are that you have faith you will come successfully through any kind of change? Do you tend to focus on what [you think] you're losing or on what you might be gaining through the change?

Now substitute the word "death" for the word "change" and consider those same questions.

Think about some of the changes you've gone through in your life, and notice what your attitude was – did you go "kicking and screaming"? Did you resign yourself and just give in? Did you accept and welcome the change as the beginning of a new and exciting chapter of your life? Did you assume things would be worse or better after the change, and what turned out to be the case? Just notice what's true, without judging yourself or your answers.

Although I don't identify myself as a Buddhist, as I've been learning more about Buddhism, I see that many of its tenets and practices make sense to me and empower me. A big part of the teachings concerns *impermanence* and *non-attachment*: first we have to realize that – actually – nothing is permanent . . . everything is changing all the time. Our belief that things don't change or that we can keep things the same is a complete illusion. And for that reason, cultivating non-attachment becomes very important ...

26

learning to let go of our attachment – to things, to people or relationships, to situations, to all the things we'd like to think are solid and unchanging but which are, in fact, always changing.

> *The awareness of impermanence can serve*
> *to deepen our commitment to living a life*
> *of value and meaning.*
> Joan Halifax, <u>Being with Dying</u>

By "non-attachment" I don't mean relinquishing our commitments to people or pretending not to care. What I mean is more like allowing things to be or change as they need to, releasing the "death grip" we sometimes have on things that we really like and hope won't change, or on things being a particular way and only that way.

Sitting safe in my cottage, looking out at the woods, it's easy for me to realize and accept the cycles of life, death, and rebirth "out there" – the leaves fall to the forest floor, they decompose and rot and become food for the seeds that fall and begin to grow there – no problem, it's all part of nature, and nature works well, right? But to see and accept that about *my* all-important life?

And my body! What does it mean that virtually all the cells and structures of my body die and regenerate themselves over the course of 7 years – I have a completely new body every 7 years? Some types of cells actually die and are replaced every 3 days! Change is constant – happening every instant to everything and everybody – no matter how static or solid things seem to be to our eyes and minds.

27

And there are other changes happening all the time – somewhat easier to see these last couple of years – old structures, economies, governments, and seemingly intractable world situations are shifting or falling apart. And, as much as we might long for "the old days" or hope that things are going to get "back to normal", new structures are taking their places; there's a new "normal" now. Do we hunker down and try to ignore it, or do we accept it and participate in co-creating what's next? Those are questions to ask ourselves about our own changing, ageing, and dying.

Working on our attitudes toward change, accepting the fact of impermanence, and cultivating non-attachment not only helps us face the prospect of dying, but also gives us more freedom throughout our lives.

Relaxing with the present moment, relaxing with hopelessness, relaxing with death, not resisting the fact that things end, that things pass, that things have no lasting substance, that everything is changing all the time – that is the basic message.
Pema Chödrön, *When Things Fall Apart*

Fear of the Unknown

For many of us, the fear seems to come from not knowing what happens during death and afterwards. What will it feel like? How scary will it be? Where will I go? Do I just disappear? What if (fill in the blank) ?

28

What does that mean about this life and about who I am?

In perhaps the first book of its kind, <u>Life After Life</u>, 1975, Raymond Moody interviewed a large number of people who had had what he called "Near Death Experiences" (NDEs): extraordinary experiences during an accident or a life-threatening illness. In many cases they were in comas or even pronounced "dead" by medical professionals and then, somehow, came back to life. A majority of these folks had uncannily similar experiences while they were "gone"; and this was before the concept of NDEs was popular or widely discussed, so it's not likely that their experiences or reports had been influenced by other people's stories.

Most of them experienced being "out of their bodies" or without a body – maybe they felt as if they were floating around near the ceiling, looking down upon their own bodies, hearing conversations family members were having way out of earshot of their hospital room. Many of them reported moving down a kind of long hallway or tunnel, with friends and family members who had already died on either side, welcoming them. And at the end of the hallway/tunnel or, in many cases, all around them from the beginning, was a white light or light-being of such brilliance, warmth, and love, that they experienced nothing but love, bliss, ecstasy, and healing.

29

For most of them, something or someone called them back – either a sense of, or the hearing of actual words telling them, "you're not finished yet, you have to go back", whereupon they were pulled back into their bodies and came back into this life.

In general, these people reported no fear moving toward this light; in fact they felt completely loved and embraced and were happy to be moving closer to the light, feeling as if they were going "home"; many of them were extremely sad to have been called from that, back to this life.

Many books have since been written, and much research is being done about these near-death experiences . . . what do they suggest about death and what comes after?

I decided to find out about this phenomenon from people I could actually talk to myself. Fortunately, two friends – Karina and Sperry – were happy to tell me about their experiences, which I share with you here.

A few years ago Karina – a woman in her 50's just getting through a really difficult period in her life – was involved in a horrific car crash. What she has been able to remember about the time of the impact was a lot of noise and chaos, and a rush of panic as she realized she couldn't breathe. At that moment, she felt that someone – some kind of *being of light* – was there with her, and she let go into unconsciousness for three days.

While she was unconscious, she experienced being completely bathed in a warm, healing, pinkish-orange pearlescent light – bathed in divine, unconditional love. She did not feel separate from anything – she was *everything* – and it was a totally blissful experience.

On the 3rd day, Karina felt pulled by the voices of her two daughters who had just come into the room, and she deliberately chose to leave this experience of blissful unity in order to be there for her daughters. She recalls it as a clear – but very difficult – decision.

The first two years of healing were challenging, physically and emotionally; but the experience she'd had had opened a door for her – she'd had a glimpse of the beautiful experience that dying is, as well as the healing being who was with her and whose presence she often feels to this day. She knew she had to surrender to her new physical limitations and allow herself to be cared for, which her near-death experience showed her she always would be.

Karina's near-death experience influences how she lives every day – she doesn't "sweat the small stuff" nearly as much; she remembers that she chose to be here; and – although it was definitely heavenly where she was – she appreciates her moments here more than before the accident.

Like most of us, Karina hopes her death won't be prolonged or unnecessarily painful, but she has no fear of dying anymore. She knows it will be an indescribably beautiful experience *and* that who she really is – her essence or energy – doesn't actually die, but continues to exist.

Sperry was 4 years old when he experienced death. His maternal grandfather was an eye, ear, nose and throat doctor in Kentucky with debilitating Parkinson's disease. To save face, he committed suicide when Sperry was 2. Through her shame and social isolation, his maternal grandmother took her own life two years later.

As Sperry was still deeply bonded with his mom, her parents' suicides made her hide her grief, trying to spare him her pain. Some days after the second death, he was out in the woods behind their home, playing the role of Zorro, his hero from TV, hoping he could save the day. On a dead tree which had recently fallen over, he climbed up and – instead of crawling like a child – he slowly and boldly walked out onto the limb. Suddenly the branch began to break underneath him. As he fell, his mind raced, grasping at what he could do to save himself from harm. It came to him to catch hold of the limb as he'd seen Zorro do, so as to "swing onto the next rooftop". Instead, the branch came down – with its full weight – on his heart. He was "gone" for 7 hours.

Sperry became free of thought, emotion, sensation and intuition. He realized his deathless "Self": an awareness free of all forms, without boundary, beginning or end – consciousness aware of itself, with no object of any kind.

Because he was so young when this happened, Sperry returned from this placeless place to feelings of ease, insight, joy and wisdom. Yet, though he saw that life was one and indivisible, it was mystifying what other people were "doing" or why. His parents, older sister

32

and younger brother were so identified with countless fears, desires and seemingly senseless concerns.

It was years before he could express it. He had seen who we truly are and that we do not die . . . that there was no *Sperry* to die! This knowing – that is in no way dependent upon knowledge – has continued to this day, allowing him to explore the unknown as his livelihood. It has certainly been – as you can well imagine – dismaying at times, as he did his best to deeply share this experience with his family, friends and co-workers. He saw how many of us "believe our minds" and how we can cling to our emotional reactions and material possessions. He has known firsthand who – and what – we all are, that our minds and bodies are only a very small piece of an eternal present within a much, much larger, unlimited peace.

What strikes me about the majority of these reports of NDEs is the similarity of experience, the fact that they point to a literally enjoyable process: people experience themselves as limitless; they experience bliss, joy, and a sense of returning "home". These stories can give us comfort, can help us have less fear.

In a recently-published book, <u>Proof of Heaven</u>, neurosurgeon Dr. Eben Alexander shares his own near-death experience. What makes his report so interesting is that he – like many people skeptical about whether these experiences tell us anything about actual death – had always insisted that the experiences were simply activity in the brain that produced what the people reported. However, when he became very ill with a neurological infection that he is sure rendered his brain inactive and *still* had one of

33

these amazing experiences, he became convinced – not only that they are real, but that they are indicative of what actually happens to us when we die.

Consider this: before a baby is born – when she's still in the womb – she's cozy, warm, and comfortable, her needs are taken care of, she's probably quite content with her life as it is in there, right? So, once she has outgrown her environment and it's time for her to move out, we (those of us waiting for her on "the other side") know that she is coming into her life, and oh, what a beautiful experience it is! However, in *her* experience . . . suddenly, things are getting really uncomfortable, she feels squished by a terrible pressure, something's pushing her, squeezing her into this unbelievably skinny tunnel, and some lady is screaming – it could be that baby feels like the world is coming to an end, and she's dying!

What if what we call "dying" is actually a "birth" into something or someplace else – another "life" or state of being – the vastness of who we really are? What if we tried simply shifting our viewpoint from our current location inside the "womb" of *this* life to a larger view, in which death is a transition of some kind – and a joyful one, at that? How might that change our fear of and resistance to the dying process itself?

Religion and spirituality, of course, can play a major role in what we think happens through death and afterwards. Some belief systems give us comfort, some have us wondering whether we've been good enough – will I go to heaven or hell? What are heaven and hell, anyway?

Hell is a disease in the human mind. The whole world is a hospital . . . We don't need to wait to go to heaven until we die . . . we have to get there before we die. It is far easier to leave the dream of hell while we are living than it is after we are dead. Between us and freedom from hell, one of our traps is our own self-importance, with its pride and its fear of shame and punishment.

Mary Carroll Nelson, <u>Beyond Fear: The Teachings of Don Miguel Ruiz</u>

Who am I, really? Is there a divine presence? Is it inside me or outside of me?

There is a vast and growing worldwide movement toward Unity Consciousness – the understanding that we are all connected, there is only one . . . anything. And I don't mean just in a philosophical way. Since the time of Einstein there has been more and more evidence from [Quantum] Science that we are literally – physically – connected; there is no "empty space", we all exist in a kind of "cosmic soup" – a "matrix" – which connects us all, and through which every action any of us takes affects the whole. As Deepak Chopra said in an interview I saw recently:

We are not just connected – we are <u>inseparable!</u>

Linked to this view is the understanding that consciousness is matter, and matter doesn't disappear, it only changes form. Am I matter? Am I consciousness? Can I disappear, or can I only change form? Again – who or what am I in these questions,

35

anyway?   Certainly Sperry's experience of death, above, points to the boundless-ness, beginning-less-ness and endlessness of who we really are.

A recent favorite book of mine is Thich Nhat Hanh's <u>No Death, No Fear: Comforting Wisdom for Life</u>.   This is a beautifully-written, simple but powerful, elaboration on the notion that we are not each a separate *thing* in a world of other things, we are not separate from nature or other people or God.   There is no separation – there is only all-that-is.   We're not going to go into this deeply in this book, and it really requires and deserves the rich explanation that Thich Nhat Hanh's book provides.   I highly recommend it.

In an interview of Rupert Sheldrake which is part of the upcoming film "Death Makes Life Possible", Sheldrake says he believes what we experience in death is influenced by what we believe, just as what we experience in life.   Can we just choose what to believe?   Of course – we're doing it all the time!   What if we chose to believe what's most empowering and inspiring?

Consider your own beliefs . . . Where did they come from?   Do they empower you to live a life you love, or do they constrain you?   Scare you?   Let you off the hook?   Keep you from facing the reality of death?   Did you choose them, and do you "own" them?   If not, what beliefs would you like to choose now?   Do you see yourself as a co-creator of your own experience in life and in death?   Part of all there is, or a separate individual at the effect of forces bigger than you?

These are the kinds of questions we can ask ourselves, discuss with others, explore in the various spiritual approaches. The more we contemplate death, consciously and purposefully, the better choices we can make about how we live our lives and plan for our deaths.

Fear of Leaving Loved Ones

I see two aspects of this fear: fear for ourselves (that [we believe] we'll no longer have or be with our loved ones), and fear for them that they'll no longer have us.

The first – that we'll no longer have them – is one of the "realities" that I question, since it isn't clear that we actually disappear when we die. Although I realize not everyone will agree with me, I believe it's possible we will still be able to experience being with our loved ones, OR that we will be in such an expansive state (as reported by people who've had NDEs) that we won't care in the same way we do as humans in this life. With that line of thinking, this aspect of the fear belongs in the category of Fear of the Unknown or What Happens After We Die, which we've just been exploring.

The second – that they'll no longer have us – has, I believe, three parts: (1) we're sad about their sadness; (2) we'll no longer be able to provide whatever we've been providing for them; and (3) there may be unfinished business regarding the relationships themselves, communication, history together, etc.

37

If our loved ones realize that we are not afraid of death, that we've lived our lives fully and have left as little unfinished business as possible, might they not be quite as sad themselves? I'm not saying we can tie everything up with a neat little bow, but if we make a point of addressing any unfinished business between us, as well as the legal, financial, and practical aspects related to end of life, we can help ourselves and our loved ones to be as ready, emotionally, as possible.

Do not stand at my grave and weep
I am not there. I do not sleep.

I am a thousand winds that blow.
I am the diamond glint on snow.

I am the sunlight on ripened grain.
I am the gentle autumn rain.

When you wake in the morning hush
I am the swift, uplifting rush
of quiet birds in circling flight.
I am the soft starlight at night.

Do not stand at my grave and weep.
I am not there. I do not sleep.

by Joyce Fossen
from Earth Prayers from Around the World

Dissatisfaction About Life Now

It's hard to feel optimistic about dying fulfilled when we're dissatisfied with our life as it is now. If I'm unhappy now and I don't want to die unhappy, I may have to make some changes, take some steps, probably face some fears and take some risks.

If it's fear that's stopping us, we can work on that. If we have unfinished business, we can work on that (and we will, later on in this book). If we know what would make us happy, we can start taking steps toward that vision; if we *don't* know, we can work on *that*! Everything is possible, especially when we really take seriously that we're going to die, this is the life we have, we are the ones dying at the end of our lives, and we need to take charge if we haven't already.

Every once in a while I realize I've had an (unconscious) belief or internal "conversation" that I'll be happy *when . . .* when this debt is paid off or I lose 20 pounds or I find the right relationship or lose the one I have . . . Once I finally catch myself, I realize what a trap this is. I'm basically telling myself I can't be happy now, and my happiness is in the future, which means it's imaginary, in a way, since the future is never actually here! My plan might be disguised as optimism or hope, but where do those end and denial begins?

What if I could be *present* to the current moment and satisfied in the current moment, no matter what the circumstances are, even if the circumstances I've always believed would make me happy don't ever come to pass? We'll explore the practice of Being Present in the chapter "5 Practices for More Conscious Living and Dying".

Resignation

Another attitude some people have about death – or about life, *because* of the inevitability of death – is resignation

There is a kind of resignation that comes with being human. It's not a personal resignation . . . I believe it's more a function of our not understanding how powerful we are, or of our feeling separate from or less powerful than all that is, nature, God, the evolutionary creative impulse . . . however we might think about it.

When I can see what it is I feel resigned about, tease it apart and uncover the underlying fear or sadness or feeling of powerlessness, I can then begin to address and resolve it. But resignation is one of those things that is sometimes hard to see – like water to the fish – so first I have to see it, second I have to believe I can resolve it, and third I have to take action in that direction.

When talking or thinking about death, some people tend to say "well, there's nothing I can do about it, so there's no use talking about it" – let's take a good look at what's underneath that statement. Maybe they're truly at peace about dying, and if so, I'd say "congratulations!"

But it might be that they haven't made the distinction between what can and cannot be controlled about death, and maybe they don't know what to do about the aspects of dying over which they *do* have control. As you can imagine, this is all part of the purpose of this book, and we will address it in "Mining the Gold - Working with What Comes Up".

It may take some work, but the work is definitely doable. There are so many resources for us to engage in this work: books, seminars, therapy, and practices to adopt – some of which we'll explore a bit later.

A Word About Depression

I'd like to make a distinction between the kind of resignation that is resolvable and the illness called Depression. I speak about this because depression is way more common than most people realize; it can be utterly debilitating; people who have it don't tend to realize they have it; a lot of people have negative opinions about it or about people (even themselves) who have it; and it's very seldom recognized for what it is – a physiological, as well as psychological, illness that can be treated.

I'm not talking about the way we feel "down" sometimes or go through challenging periods in an otherwise happy existence . . . I'm talking about a pervasive feeling of hopelessness, resignation, powerlessness, an inability to experience pleasure, lack of interest in just about anything . . . symptoms you can learn about easily using resources like the Internet, or by talking with your doctor.

Depression can be temporary or chronic; it can be treated by therapy/counseling and with medication, natural supplements, and other modalities, like yogic breathing, for example. It's important to realize there is no shame in having depression . . . it's only a "shame" that many people suffer with it (as I did) for years, thinking there is something fundamentally wrong with their character, when in fact they may have a correctable chemical imbalance and/or old, unresolved and unconscious experiences from the past that can be safely and relatively painlessly brought to the surface and resolved with the help of a good therapist. If you think you might have depression, I really encourage you to check it out.

That being said, we are all subject – at different times in our lives and to varying degrees – to a mood of resignation about what's possible and how much power we have in our lives, and whether we let the reality of death limit us or liberate us. That's why recognizing the resignation and working to resolve it can have such a powerful positive impact for our lives.

Superstition

Even talking about death is considered morbid [in the West], and many people believe that simply mentioning death is to risk wishing it upon ourselves.
Sogyal Rinpoche, *The Tibetan Book of Living and Dying*

As you can tell from how I have labeled this reason for not talking about death, I don't believe it is possible to hasten your death by talking about it. I do believe that we influence our lives enormously by whatever we repeatedly say or focus on, so it actually helps to think about, discuss, or focus on the possibility of dying with as much consciousness and aliveness as possible . . . that's largely what this book is about. So don't be afraid to authentically talk about death and your concerns and desires about how you make that most important transition in your life. After all – it's your life, and you'll be the one going through that process at the end of it.

Journaling Questions! * Why Don't We Talk About Death?

- In what ways am I in denial about death – my own or that of others?

- What do I tell myself about death?

- What am I afraid of with regard to death?

- What am I worried about?

- What do I feel resigned about?

- Where do I "hold back" in my life because of fear?

- What might I have to believe in order for death to be less fearsome to me?

- What about death (or life) am I curious about?

- How could I investigate those things?

- What do I feel about the possibility of dying consciously?

- Assuming I have some control over my death, how would I want it to be?

Why Should We Talk About Death?

Our fears don't stop death, they stop life.
Elisabeth Kübler-Ross & David Kessler, Life
Lessons

I have come to realize that the disastrous
effects of the denial of death go far beyond
the individual: they affect the whole
planet . . . modern people have developed
no long-term vision. So there is nothing to
restrain them from plundering the planet
for their own immediate ends and from
living in a selfish way that could prove
fatal for the future.
Sogyal Rinpoche, The Tibetan Book of Living
and Dying

What People Say at the End of Their Lives

Whether from personal experience or things that we've heard or read, we're all familiar with some of the things people say when they realize they're dying. Here's a potpourri of what I've heard over the years:

- I wish I hadn't worked so hard.

- I wish I'd had more courage to be myself and not care so much what other people think or expect.

- I wish I'd expressed my love more, or let myself be loved more.

- I wish I'd been less fearful.

- I wish I'd been more generous.

- I wish I/we'd taken that trip I/we always wanted to take.

- I wish I'd started/stopped (fill in the blank) earlier.

I don't think anyone's been quoted as saying "I should have spent more time at work, making money, accumulating stuff", and yet these are precisely the things we make so important in our lives, the things we focus on while putting off our dreams, putting off the things we may one day realize were most important.

I love what Apple co-founder Steve Jobs said, shortly before he died in 2011:

> *Remembering that I'll be dead soon is the most important tool I've ever encountered to help me make the big choices in life. Because almost everything — all external expectations, all pride, all fear of embarrassment or failure — these things just fall away in the face of death, leaving only what is truly important. Remembering that you are going to die is the best way I know to avoid the trap of thinking you have something to lose. You are already naked. There is no reason not to follow your heart.*

What if we didn't wait until we knew we were dying to adopt this approach to life?   Or what if we acknowledged that we already are dying – we're *always* already dying . . . we just don't know how long we have? Kind of makes some of our fears about expressing ourselves and taking everyday risks look a little silly, doesn't it? Jobs' quote articulates beautifully that it is possible for the reality of death to motivate us to live a life we love, to help us clear away the "fluff" and recognize what's important to us – now, not later (when it's too late).

The goal is not to be *happy* about dying! And I don't pretend that – having read this book – you should have no fears or concerns left about death.

Our goals in looking at death and what comes up when we do could be as follows:

- To become aware of our fears so that we can practice acceptance of what we can't change and take action on what we can

- To learn what is currently incomplete for ourselves, so that we can have as little unfinished business – personal, interpersonal, and practical – as possible . . . at all times, and especially at the time of our death

- To be as free, present, and grateful as possible, in every moment of our life and death

48

The Power of Awareness

What this book is really about is becoming aware of how we feel and what we believe about death, so that we can examine those feelings or beliefs and determine whether they really serve us, or that maybe we'd be more empowered by different ones. It's about the possibility of living – and dying – more consciously.

Aren't we always aware of what we feel or believe and the actions those feelings and beliefs lead us to take? Well . . . no, we're not.

Each of us has what might be called a worldview, which we sometimes consciously create for ourselves, but which often exists and is operating without our conscious awareness.

What is a worldview? My worldview is the lens through which I see the world, the "filter" through which the world passes even before it enters my awareness. Imagine you're wearing colored glasses – if your glasses are yellow, then the world looks yellow to you, everything has a yellowish tint to your eyes. When you take the glasses off, you can see that the sky isn't *really* green, but is colored by the glasses before its light hits your eyes.

The thing is, most of us are not aware of our worldview . . . we just think that's really the way the world is; we don't usually ask ourselves (1) might I have colored glasses on? or (2) what color are they? In other words – what are the beliefs (inherited or developed along the way), assumptions, biases, desires, hopes, fears, and decisions from past experiences that are coloring and filtering how I see and assess everything?

This may seem like an easy thing to recognize, but this, too, is like asking a fish to look at the water it's swimming in – *what water?* It doesn't see any water! Unless and until the fish jumps or is pulled out of the water and looks down at it, it has no idea whether it's clear or muddy or green, blue, or black; it has no idea that there's something outside of what it thought was everything. Water to a fish is like air to a bird: invisible and yet all-important, the way our beliefs are to us.

We can't see our worldview unless we back up, take our glasses off and try to examine them objectively, to discover what is coloring what we see and how differently things might appear without those particular glasses.

One day in my twenties, I was watching a movie about two people amazingly in love; it really captured my heart; then the man died (yes – just like that). In that moment, I suddenly had a memory of watching such a movie as a very young girl, and deciding – without being aware of my decision – that there's no sense really falling in love with someone, since they're just going to die anyway! Wow – talk about resignation. The realization that I had this worldview was shocking at first. However, it helped me understand how I had behaved in some of my relationships up until that point, as you can imagine. It also gave me the opportunity to examine that belief and see if I wanted to hang on to it or create a new one.

Why is it important to be aware of our worldview, and to practice catching ourselves with our colored glasses on?

1. Until we have awareness of what worldview is operating in our life at any given moment, *it* is "operating" *us*, while we continue to believe we are seeing things "as they are" – seeing what's possible – when, in fact, there could be whole worlds of possibility available to us that those particular glasses are filtering out, not allowing us to see. With awareness, we then have the opportunity to choose new glasses.

2. How we do or approach anything tends to be how we do or approach *everything*. Once you uncover a fear or limiting belief you didn't know was operating in your life, you'll probably discover that it's been operating in other areas of your life, too.

In the example above of the unconscious belief I had about falling in love . . . once I realized I had resignation about that, I could see that I had a sense of resignation in other parts of life, too, and that I'd been operating as if "that's just the way life is". That allowed me to work on letting go of the resignation – either working on my own or with the help of other resources – so that I could experience more freedom and happiness in my life.

Some people refer to our filters as our "listening" . . . when I listen to or read (a kind of listening) something, what am I listening *with*? What am I listening *for*, what am I listening *to* inside my own head? This is a kind of auditory description of our filters, where worldview is a kind of visual description.

If you're having a hard time noticing what your *listening* is, notice the conversation going on in your head right at this moment. (Hint: if you're currently thinking something like "what conversation is she talking about?" . . . that's exactly the conversation I'm talking about.) It's a running commentary, kind of like your own internal sports commentator, making comments on everything that comes into your awareness – judging, sorting, believing, disbelieving, liking, disliking, and so on.

Sometimes we take action or make decisions based on this voice – as if we assume it's the voice of God or some other "authority". Or we figure everybody has that "angel" on one shoulder and "devil" on the other that we've seen in cartoons – and that life is naturally the constant battle between the two. The important thing is to notice the voice(s) and recognize that none of them is *who we really are*. Who we really are is much deeper and broader.

Whatever helps us see/notice/feel/hear the filters we are wearing – the filters that set up what's possible even before anything happens – we must use that to enhance our awareness. And it's good to be compassionate with ourselves, trying to just observe, rather than judge or self-criticize.

If you pay attention, you cannot fail. "All the way to heaven is heaven," said Catherine of Siena. You have already

arrived. The journey is simply to live in that awareness.
Jan Phillips, <u>No Ordinary Time</u>

** Journaling Questions! ** Why Should We Talk About Death?

Suggested exercise: writing in your journal or on a piece of paper, start practicing noticing your own filters.   You can use what you've read so far as material for the exercise.

- I realize I tend to bring an attitude of _____to most situations.

- Through what filters am I reading this book?

- What I have believed or assumed about death is _____.

- I have similar beliefs about _____.

- What else have I noticed so far?

5 Practices for More Conscious Living and Dying

It seems to me that consciousness leads to freedom, which leads to happiness. And by "freedom" I don't mean having no responsibility or commitments; I mean freedom to be, do, and live authentically, by one's own rules, with a deep awareness of the power each of us possesses to create our own experience, our own response to what life brings us.

There are, of course, all kinds of practices available to us; but for the purposes of this book, I'd like to highlight five practices that have been very powerful for me. I believe these same practices will also allow for the best possible experience of death:

- Taking **Ownership**

- **Surrendering**

- Being **Present**

- Being **Complete**

- Cultivating **Gratitude**

Understanding what each of these practices is and how we might cultivate them in our own lives not only enriches our experience of living but is also a useful foundation for looking at and working with what comes up when we do the exercise on "Imagining Death – an Ancient Practice". When we do that exercise, to the degree that we can make use of these, it should be clearer what actions we'll want to take and how to go through the follow-on exercises – both in this book experience and in the rest of life.

For me, these practices are fundamental and extremely important, and they are developed and honed over a lifetime. Although even a few "drops" of any of them can make an immediate impact on our lives whenever we first engage with them, there will always be opportunities to deepen our relationship to them and integrate them more and more fully into who we naturally are.

I acknowledge that there's some overlap among these practices, and I believe that's because they are all related, interconnected . . . in developing one, we naturally also touch on others.

I would like to distinguish between *tools* (some of which we will uncover in the chapter on "Mining the Gold - Working with What Comes Up") and *practices*. I think of a tool as something tangible and practical that one can use and apply for immediate results. A practice is a concept, idea, or approach that we actually practice, make our own, and become more adept with over time.

Taking Ownership

Other ways of expressing *Taking Ownership*:

- Developing and expanding awareness on a continual basis

- Taking responsibility for [my response to] what happens in my life

- Becoming aware of, and accepting (ultimately without shame, blame, or guilt) my part in what shows up in my life

- Realizing the power and impact of my thoughts and attitudes on my reality

- Giving myself – locating within myself – the authority to determine who I am, what I do, and how I live my life

- Knowing I always have choice

- Not being a victim

Since I have a feeling the last one is most prone to misunderstanding, let's be clear . . . We usually define "victim" as someone to whom some wrongdoing has been committed – someone who has been hurt or wronged in some way. Referring to that person as the victim of the act or crime is an accepted use of the word "victim", which is *not* what I'm referring to here.

When I speak of "not being a victim" as a practice, I'm referring to victimhood as a kind of posture, or stance, in the world . . . the relationship one has with the world, with life. We all know people who constantly see and talk about themselves as victims – almost no matter what – right? These are the easy ones to spot – it's always someone else's fault, they never seem to "own up" to what they've done to create the mess they're complaining about, etc. And we've all heard ourselves take the victim posture, even if only for a moment. I know I have.

Sometimes it's actually tempting to act the victim – we get sympathy, people don't expect as much from us, it's a lot easier (in some ways) to believe that we have less power than we do, especially when things around us are looking yucky. We do it as a culture, too, when we identify "us" as the good guys and "them" as the bad guys who are "doing it to us again!" There's a strong pull – when things aren't going well – to look for someone or something else to blame.

The problem with acting the victim, or taking the victim stance, is that it leaves us powerless. We build a little cage for ourselves, and we're stuck there, because we can't be a victim and have power at the same time. Even people who have truly experienced being victimized in some real way have the choice whether to take on victimhood as a way of life or take back their own power . . . take back ownership of their lives.

Everything can be taken from [us] but one thing: the last of the human freedoms – to choose one's attitude in any given set of circumstances, to choose one's own way"
Viktor Frankl (Nazi Concentration Camp Survivor), Man's Search for Meaning

Whether or not you believe in "God" is a very personal thing, of course. Still, consider the difference between thinking of God as a "controller" or parental figure outside yourself (not part of you) and thinking of God as being within you, part of you and/or you as part of God . . . do you feel a different sense of responsibility and ownership in one versus the other?

Authenticity expresses another aspect of Taking Ownership. To think for ourselves and live authentically, even when other people may think we're crazy; to speak our authentic truth, especially when others think it would be safer, easier, or more polite to stay silent. In my experience, it takes courage, but it's worth it to be able to say, at the end of the day (or the life) that we were true to ourselves – our *real* self . . . that our choices were our own.

Realizing the power of our thoughts and attitudes to affect what happens in our lives, including death, this – as well as most of the practices and ideas of this chapter – is something that can be pointed and alluded to; we can come up with examples; we can share resources for developing it – books, workshops, ongoing practices, affirmations, etc. But the way to make any of these practices our own is to (1) see and be inspired by the possibility of it, and (2) commit to

58

developing it within ourselves. No quick or easy fixes, although I must say it's helpful to me to have frequent reminders and to hang around (loving and supportive) others with similar commitments.

There are different ways to approach this practice of Taking Ownership – philosophical, practical, scientific, educational – which you might want to explore. Look into some of the explanations of Quantum Physics and how we are all literally connected (I look for the explanations for the "non-scientist" – for example, presentations by Amit Goswami, Michio Kaku, or Lynne McTaggart); take a workshop that helps you see your worldview or hear your listening.

Anything that helps us increase our awareness of ourselves and our unconscious motivators, and gives us a glimpse of the possibilities and freedom available (but often invisible) to us at every moment, can be exciting and empowering. It can help us live more fully and die with less regret, less remorse, and less unfinished business.

Surrendering

Other ways of expressing *Surrendering*:

- Allowing

- Embracing / Choosing / Not resisting *what is*

- Letting go of control, of "being right", of my "position"

- Giving up attachment to things being a certain way

- Being vulnerable (e.g., admitting I was wrong, identifying and sharing emotions that might be difficult for me)

Ah – surrender! For me, this is one of the most immediately powerful *and* difficult of the practices.

Over the years, most of us have built up such a strong need to be right, to feel in control, to take a position and not budge from it. These are very common responses to life. And ironically – the more we feel threatened or insecure – the more we're likely to stick to our guns, stand fast on our position, insist on "my way or the highway". For whatever reason(s), we (who we think we are) would almost rather die than give in . . . sound familiar?

One of the first things to remember, when I find myself holding on so tightly to something (and it's clearly not working, in terms of having what I really want – relationship, happiness, workability), is that who I really am is not my position; I really am not going to die if I let go. Who I think I am in that moment might have to "die" in a sense – but not who I really am.

This kind of "death" is obviously not the same as really dying. But in the moment that I have a death grip on my position or my need to be in control, it sure can feel like it.

That's why every opportunity to surrender is an opportunity to experience that who I *really* am doesn't die.

The more we practice it, the easier it gets. Start with relatively non-threatening things, like whatever silly thing you find yourself arguing about with your spouse or friend. As you get the hang of it – and start to see the enormous benefits – you can try it with things that feel more important – something that you think really *is* who you are!

One of the exciting things about the practice of surrender is that you can practice it all by yourself. It isn't just other people who can make us feel threatened – it can be . . .

- **Feelings** (e.g., fear, anger, sadness, boredom, shame, embarrassment, even love)

- **Thoughts** (for example, I can't, I don't want to, I don't deserve it, they'll laugh at me)

- **Circumstances** in which we feel out of control or out of our comfort zone e.g., illness or disabilities (even minor or temporary), almost any unexpected or unwanted situation

In one situation, surrender might look like acknowledging what I'm feeling and just allowing it to be, no longer resisting it, and giving myself the chance to find out what might be behind or underneath that feeling. If I'm with someone else – it might be to acknowledge to the other person what I'm feeling (even though I feel embarrassed, I don't know how they're going to respond, i.e., I'm letting go of control); the result – if I'm being authentic about it and not just trying a technique to get myself out of an uncomfortable situation (still trying to be in control) – will probably be a pleasant surprise that will deepen my relationship with the other person and with myself.

Here's a somewhat simplistic test you can try: if you find yourself thinking or feeling something like "NO, not *that* – anything but that!" you've probably found the perfect thing with which to experiment surrendering.

An example from my life: in my twenties and thirties, I remember that boredom was the feeling I dreaded most. I hated being bored! And, not surprisingly, it seemed to happen a *lot* . . .

What you resist persists.
Erhard Seminars Training

One day, when I was first learning about the possibility of surrender, I decided to stop resisting the boredom and just be bored . . . just to see what would happen (I figured I could handle it and besides – anything would be better than being bored). So – I didn't do any of the things I would usually do automatically when I was bored – eat, drink, watch TV, doodle, play solitaire, take a nap; I just lay down on the couch and let myself experience boredom. I noticed the urges to do the automatic things, but rather than give in to them, I just let the urges be; they soon passed. As I continued to lie there, I began to notice the tension in my body and the shallowness of my breathing; so I let go of some of the tension and started breathing more deeply, slowly, actually enjoying the feelings that produced in my body. Suddenly I realized I wasn't bored anymore! I was relaxed and in touch with my body, and I felt like going for a walk.

Try it out – next time you're by yourself and a feeling comes up that you usually resist – for many people it's anger, maybe because in their family anger wasn't allowed or was present and was such a scary thing they decided to ban it from their lives, or fear, or sadness – instead of doing the things you usually do to make the feeling go away, just allow it to be. Become very curious about it. Try to feel it *more*. Just notice the feeling without judging either it or yourself, and see what happens.

Another clue that it might be time to practice surrendering is when you hear yourself saying or thinking "this isn't supposed to happen, it's not how it's supposed to be". Here's a common one: "I thought I had already dealt with this!" Something helpful that one of my grad school teachers offered is to imagine personal development and growth as a *spiral* rather than the straight line we tend to imagine . . . as you go around the spiral, you're always moving upwards; and sometimes, your spiral comes back around through "that same old issue". The important thing to notice is that you are in a different place this time, and it is always so; so it's never really the same old issue, and you're never really the "same old you".

Here's a tool for such situations – it came from a workshop with Werner Erhard & Associates years ago . . . When we are upset about something, or we hear ourselves thinking "it's not supposed to be this way", there usually is one, two, or all three of the following at work:

- an undelivered communication

- a thwarted intention

- an unfulfilled expectation

Applying this tool is really helpful, because just the act of remembering to use the tool gives us back some power and puts the situation in front of us rather than all round us or on top of us. In other words, we change our relationship to the situation. The tool is simple, and it's effective.

Look at the situation and determine – is there something not being said that could make a difference (usually something I need to say)? Did I have an intention, an "agenda" – something I was trying to make happen – that isn't happening (and do I need to communicate about that or just surrender)? Was I expecting something, or am I realizing *they* were expecting something, that didn't happen, about which we might need to communicate?

We'll be using this tool later, in the chapter "Mining the Gold - Working with What Comes Up" – we'll call it the "What's So" tool. It's very helpful in cleaning up upsets, identifying what needs to be said, to whom, and what we need to let go.

The power of the practice of not resisting what's so is mind-blowing. Think about how much time and energy you spend not wanting something to be the way it is; imagine (1) getting all that time and energy back and (2) feeling the new feelings and possibilities that arise once you've stopped resisting.

Have you ever noticed how quickly the time seems to fly when you're happy, enjoying yourself, or totally engrossed in something (i.e., not resisting)? And how it drags when you're doing something you don't want to do – something you're resisting?

This takes us back to the victim conversation . . . when I'm experiencing something as unwanted, unfair, not supposed to be this way, etc., that experience or situation feels bigger or more powerful than me, in a way (which is one way to describe the *victim* position). When I can look at it, name it, and allow it, I am suddenly bigger than it, because I'm able to *see* it – I'm no longer in it, I'm outside of it, observing it. It feels completely different; now I can notice what else becomes visible or possible. I might actually start to feel curious about it.

American Buddhist nun Pema Chödrön expresses so clearly our tendency to resist or avoid pain and suffering. I love the authenticity and raw honesty of her words; it's as if she somehow sees right into me.

This makes me realize, once again, how connected we all are, how similar our struggles are as human beings, and how futile it is to try to avoid pain and difficulty.

The practice of Insight or Mindfulness Meditation, though seemingly very simple, is a powerful tool for learning to surrender to life as it is, in every moment. In fact, many of the Buddhist teachings apply to all of us as human beings. I like how accessible these teachings are, and that they don't conflict with any existing religious or spiritual practices we might have – it's more about learning to accept fully what it means to be human, on a very practical and practicable level.

A few last words about Surrendering . . .

- It is often preceded by Taking Ownership

- It is not the same as giving up or giving away your power or succumbing, in the sense of being or feeling like a victim or a martyr. However, sometimes giving up the struggle against something is in itself an act of power, and it usually brings with it a sense of freedom and relief.

- It usually requires taking a leap of faith . . . that what I'm letting go of is holding me/the situation back and what I'm letting go *into* will offer bigger, more workable, more life-affirming possibilities.

- It can't be "faked".

- It gets easier with practice.

Being Present

If you want to know where God, the Buddhas and all the great beings live, I can tell you. Here is their address: in the here and now.
Thich Nhat Hanh, <u>No Death, No Fear</u>

Other ways of expressing *Being Present*:

- Being here, now

- Being in the [present] moment

- Paying attention to what is

- Choosing to be where you are, doing what you're doing, right now

- Loving yourself, your life, now – not needing to wait for anybody or anything to appear or change

- Letting go of past and future

- Letting go of "your agenda" or of "pictures" of how it's supposed to be

- Being open to, available for, the beauty and possibility of every moment

Spiritual teacher Ram Dass (earlier known as Dr. Richard Alpert) wrote a book in the 1970's called <u>Remember, Be Here Now</u>. It's a simple but very profound book, just as the idea of being here now is

67

also simple but profound. Simple . . . but not always *easy*. We are so conditioned to rush, try to anticipate, be prepared, put our guard up, get a million things done at once. Do we not trust ourselves to just breathe and *be* for a moment?

Think through the last 24 hours and notice how many times you were not present to what you were doing, because you were . . .

- daydreaming

- wishing you were somewhere else or doing something else

- (trying to) multi-task

- listening (sort of) to someone while thinking about what you would say next

I've often chuckled at myself rushing through traffic so I could hurry up and get to a massage or get home so I could finally relax! What if I could be present and relaxed during the drive, as well as the massage? Because – and here's the bottom line – I *could* actually die before I get to that massage.

We don't usually say this kind of thing, but that's why I wrote this book and presumably why you're reading it . . . it's the truth. But knowing the truth, in and of itself, doesn't change our habits – we have to see the potential benefits of changing, or maybe the downside of not changing, and commit to new behaviors, not wait until we know the end is near. That's almost always too late.

If we're always trying to get somewhere, what we experience of our lives will be dominated by the trying or striving – in other words – we only ever experience not being where we want to be. We never get to "somewhere", because that's always in the future. When we get to where we thought we wanted to be, we're almost never present – we're thinking, worrying, planning, regretting, strategizing, managing (ourselves, our feelings and reactions), comparing . . .

> *You are what you are looking for. You are already what you want to become . . . Take the time to look deeply into yourself and recognize that your nature is the nature of no-birth and no-death. . . This method of practice will help us to live without fear, and it will help us to die peacefully without regret.*
> Thich Nhat Hanh, No Death, No Fear

At any given moment, stop. Breathe deeply and slowly, and be exactly where you are, doing what you're doing, being with whomever you're with, all of you – 100% – in that moment. As you experiment with this powerful practice, you will see or be reminded just how life-changing it is.

Imagine – if we were able to be fully present when our partner or child is speaking to us – what might we learn? What might become possible? We might be actually seeing who they are for the first time. And what might we learn about ourselves and who we really are? Or the myriad of possibilities inherent in every single moment when we let go of preconceived ideas and agendas?

One of the first times I purposely experienced being present, I was driving on Hwy 280 (on the San Francisco Peninsula), probably replaying in my head some conversation that hadn't gone well, when I decided to just be present and pay attention to the moment I was in. Suddenly, a whole world opened up – it was as if the entire landscape had switched from black-and-white to color, and it was gorgeous! I experienced such a rush of gratitude, I had tears in my eyes. By contrast – how many times have I driven somewhere without experiencing or appreciating a single moment of the drive?

Notice that Being Present brings together aspects of all the practices we've discussed so far: Taking Ownership (of the situation in which you find yourself); Surrendering to being there; and choosing to Be Present to the moment – open to all the possibilities, open to being surprised, moved, blown away, being there without an action plan or a strategy – just present and alive.

Every moment we're able to be totally present is a richer, fuller, even *longer* moment. I believe it's what helps us know that we've lived – being present in this moment, and this moment, and this moment.

Exercise for Becoming More Present

So many of us rush around, pushing ourselves to *do* as much as possible. There are so many demands on our time – from others and from within ourselves. But

70

being is where the power is, the source of the strength and clarity for whatever we do.

Sometimes we try to *think* ourselves into being present, when *feeling* – being in touch with the more physical aspects of our being, moving out of our heads and into our hearts – can be much more effective.

> **The longest journey a person can make is from their head to their heart.**
> *(source unknown)*

Take a few moments for this:

- Sit comfortably.

- Breathe deeply.

- Notice the urge to keep moving, and let yourself stop the forward momentum . . . maybe even lean back a little.

- Focus on your breath going in and out.

- Allow whatever attention, energy, tension or thoughts that seem to be in the upper part of your body – your head, neck, jaw, throat, shoulders – settle down into the lower part of your body – your heart, belly, hips, tailbone, legs, feet.

- With every out-breath, sink more and more into your body, and relax. Let go.

- Notice that there is nothing to do in this moment; nowhere to go; nothing missing, nothing needed.

71

- Everything you need is here in this moment.

- Allow yourself to experience the utter perfection of this moment.

Being Complete

Other ways of expressing *Being Complete*:

- Nothing left unsaid or undone

- Following through on promises made – to others and to oneself

- Keeping environment (and mind) organized, uncluttered

- No loose ends, no unfinished business

- Apologies made, forgiveness experienced

It's interesting to look at the many ways that *not* being complete can show up, the many forms it can take (they're different for everybody); it's vital to be honest about the things that are incomplete in our lives and to take steps to complete them. This is true for all of life and – as you can imagine – especially at the end of life.

Completion Inventory – this is something I highly recommend doing often, and we'll certainly come back to it in the chapter "Mining the Gold - Working with What Comes Up". Every once in a while I take a look at my life – home environment, work environment, relationships (with friends, family, co-workers, neighbors, my body, my spirituality, nature), my car, finances, health – every aspect of life I can think of. I take a big sheet of paper and make a column for each aspect with its title at the top of the column.

Then I consider each aspect of my life and ask myself, "what's incomplete?" What haven't I done that I said I would do, or what have I done that I said I wouldn't do? Whom did I promise to call? What am I putting off? What's been bugging me or on my mind? And I write all these things down.

For relationships, I sometimes ask myself the question, "if they were to die before I see them again, what would I wish I had or hadn't said or done?" It's the kind of question that helps me get quickly through the fluff to the bottom line.

A couple of notes about this and any of the suggestions/processes/practices in this book:

(1) I try to use "tough love" with myself. In other words, this exercise is for me – only for me – which means if I try to "cheat", maybe no one else will know, but I also won't reap the benefit. And I emphasize the "love" part as well as the "tough" – if it's the first time I've done this inventory in a while, I might be a little overwhelmed by how many things are on my lists. I try to have patience and compassion with myself, and acknowledge myself for doing really important work.

(2) One person's incompletions might not even show up on another person's incompletions radar. What we consider incomplete has to do with our own sense and definition of integrity – wholeness, congruence – no one else's. So – while a house piled with books and papers makes me feel uneasy and unable to

74

concentrate – for you, it might be just the right kind and level of stimulation or comfort. So we have to look honestly at our own integrity, not what we think someone else would think about it.

Some sample lists:

Health
- Make eye doctor appointment

- Schedule mammogram

- Get real about walking every day [either let it go or make a more realistic promise to myself]

Friends
- Send thank-you note/Tweet to Betsy

- Respond to Joel's e-mail

- Clear up misunderstanding with Jolene

- Apologize to Barbara

Whether it's right there in my face or just barely tickling me at the back of my mind – if it comes up, I try to get it down on paper. Then I start knocking them off, realizing as I complete each one that I am clearing/cleaning out space for my soul to shine through and express itself, to lighten up as I jettison the weights – light, heavy, serious, not-so-serious – that have been cluttering my space, holding me down, keeping me from feeling completely great about myself and my life. As I make space, new things can come in. And when I practice being complete on a somewhat regular basis, I find the incompletions don't pile up as much.

I was listening to a talk about fund-raising tips from one of the best fund-raisers in the world. When she's about to lead a fund-raising event, she makes sure her *own* finances are complete: every bill is paid, all the checks are written and sent, her checkbook is balanced. She recognizes – and pays attention to – the connection between her own integrity (especially in the area of finances) and her ability to be effective in approaching people about theirs.

Do you need to agonize over whether or not to complete something? No. Just be as honest as you can with yourself – is this thing taking up space in my mind, my consciousness, my ability to be fully present? Do I think about it when I'm with that person? Does it come up as I'm falling asleep at night, or does it keep me awake? Do I curse every time I stub my toe on that pile of books? Just tell the truth and complete it . . . or let it go.

Sometimes I look at something on my list, and I realize it's just not important – it was on my mind so I put it on the list, but I'm truly willing to let it go. So I let it go. Or – if I've broken a promise to someone (including myself) – I admit that I didn't do it and either re-commit to doing it (within a specific time frame), change it to something I really am committed to doing, or acknowledge (to myself or the other person) that I'm never going to do it . . . freeing up that space between me and my friend or within myself.

It seems to me we have to stop pretending that the things we leave undone or try to ignore aren't bothering us, aren't taking up space in our psyches, aren't affecting our relationships or our ability to be effective, to be truly alive.

Maybe more importantly, we have to stop pretending that who we are doesn't make a difference . . . that incompletions in our lives affect only us, when in fact they limit who we're able to be, how much of our unique gifts we're able to share and express in the world. So, these practices are a matter of *honoring ourselves*, our uniqueness, our importance, and the importance of loving the lives we have.

Who knows what wonderful opportunities or people or ideas might come into the space we make available? And notice how Being Complete conspires with Taking Ownership, Surrendering, and Being Present to help us create our own experience of living . . . and dying.

Cultivating Gratitude

Last – but certainly not least – the practice of *Cultivating Gratitude.*

If you are naturally grateful for all you have, if you don't focus on and compare yourself with others who seem to have more than you, if you tend to talk about what you appreciate rather than what you don't like or what you don't have . . . then you are probably a joy to be around, and you probably have wonderful things happening to you all the time. I admire you!

For many of us, however, gratitude doesn't come naturally or easily – it's definitely something we have to consciously cultivate. And if we're hanging around people who always seem to complain, whine, or point out everything that isn't working, it can be especially challenging. There's plenty of what's not working to focus on, and it's usually easier to get others to agree with you that things are messed up, unfair, hopeless, out of our control, etc. It takes courage in such an environment to focus on what is working, to say I'm going to cultivate feeling grateful, on purpose.

Why cultivate an "attitude of gratitude"? Well – in addition to making us more fun for others to be around – we tend to be happier – it just feels better! And we tend to get more of whatever we're grateful for.

Maybe you've heard some of these expressions: What you focus on, you will get more of – it's a law of the universe (The Law of Attraction, for example). What you see, or look for, is what you get. What you

78

appreciate appreciates, as in grows. You're not happy because things are going well . . . things go well because you're happy!

Think of people you know who focus on what they're grateful for – does it seem as if they have a lot to be grateful for? It might be tempting to believe that they have more than we do and therefore should be grateful. But I believe it's actually the reverse – the more grateful they are, the more they focus their attention on what's working and what they have, instead of what's not working or what they don't have – the more they have and the more things will be working.

Try it with your partner, co-worker, child, or friend . . . try pointing out the things you love about them for a day, or even a conversation. What happens? They seem to magically do more of things you love about them! Is it because you're "showing them the love" and it empowers them? Probably. Is it because you've changed your glasses? Probably. Does it really matter why? I say no. Just check out how you feel, how much optimism and positive potential is there – that makes it all worthwhile.

But are we being realistic when we're focusing only on the "good" stuff? Well, it's all about choice. We can choose to be grateful for the so-called "bad" stuff, if only for the lessons it brings us. And second, whether something is "bad" or "good" is a matter of interpretation, a judgment, not inherently true, and something only we humans seem to need to assess about every person, situation, feeling, and so on.

Cultivating Gratitude makes us feel good, which empowers us, which allows us to do more of the things that make us (and others) feel good.

Lots of good books have been written on this practice, so this will be a relatively short discussion here, although we will make use of it in the chapter "Mining the Gold - Working with What Comes Up". But if you'd like to try a quick exercise: Give yourself 2 minutes and write down everything you can think of for which you're grateful. What do you notice?

Another exercise – which many people do as a daily practice – is to spend a moment just before going to sleep to write down everything from their day for which they feel grateful. It's a beautiful way to end the day and to habituate ourselves to the practice of generating gratitude.

Dr. Bernie Siegel – pioneer in exploring and reporting on the power of our minds to influence our health and well-being – shared his gratitude practice in an interview with The Shift Network. He starts each month at the beginning of the alphabet, and each morning he comes up with several things for which he's grateful that begin with that day's letter. The following month he goes back to the beginning of the alphabet. Simple, and powerful.

Having difficulty feeling grateful? For many years, I was unable to feel gratitude. In fact, these kinds of gratitude exercises really annoyed me, because I did not feel grateful to be alive. Most of the time, life felt like a big pain in the butt to me . . . it was too hard, and I believed (unconsciously) it was because something was fundamentally wrong with me or I just wasn't able to figure out the right "formula" for life. What's obvious to me now but wasn't then is that I actually had depression, as well as some very old beliefs that needed to be brought into the open, examined, and released. Once I got treated for that and did some deep work with myself, I became more and more able to feel grateful. Now I feel grateful much of the time, but I still work to remind myself often . . . what I appreciate *appreciates*.

If you are truly unable to feel grateful – or to even imagine feeling grateful – I suggest that you might want to consider getting some help. "Help" might take the form of working with a "buddy" (for this or any practice you want to develop), taking workshops, participating in therapy for a while, and/or being assessed for depression. Be assured that you would not be the only one, and nobody deserves or needs to go through life feeling ungrateful.

Journaling Questions! * 5 Practices for More Conscious Living and Dying

- Which of the suggested practices interest(s) me most at this moment?

- With which practice(s) do I have the most difficulty? Why?

- Which practice(s) do I already do? How might I become even better with it?

- What practice(s) would *I* add to the list?

Imagining Death – an Ancient Practice

So far we've looked at why we tend to not talk about death, why we tend to fear it, and why we need to talk, think and feel about it, long before we realize our moment to die has come, if we're lucky enough to have some time. And – while talking and learning about concepts and practices is good and can be useful – nothing is as impactful as our own experience of something.

> *Many traditions teach the inevitability of death as the bedrock for the entire spiritual path. Plato told his students, "Practice dying." The Christian monks of medieval Europe ritually whispered to one another, "Memento mori" ("Remember death"). And one Buddhist sutra [teaching] tells us, "Of all footprints, that of the elephant is supreme. Of all meditations, that on death is supreme."*
> Joan Halifax, <u>Being with Dying</u>

Let's do a simplified version of the practice now.

You know you're safe, you can stop this exercise whenever you want, you're in charge, and the whole next chapter gives practices, tools, and suggestions on how to deal with what comes up during this exercise.

So – please do the following:

- Create a comfortable environment for yourself where you won't be interrupted for at least 30 minutes. You might want to light a candle, have some soft or inspiring music playing – whatever makes this a special or even sacred experience for you.

- Have with you a notebook, journal, or paper, and something to write with.

- Sit in a comfortable position.

- Now, imagine you suddenly realize you're going to die, maybe even in the next few moments.

- Allow yourself to become present and stay present to the moment and the thoughts and feelings that arise.

- Write down everything that comes up – not in long sentences, but in whatever kind of shorthand will allow you to get it all down on paper.

In case you'd like some help getting started, see if the following examples help and fill in the blanks or complete the sentences:

Fear –
What about . . . ?
What if . . . ?

Who'll take care of . . . ?
I'm afraid . . .
I hope . . .

Other Emotions –
I'm angry that . . .
I'm sad that . . .
I'm happy that . . .
I'm relieved that . . .

Resistance – NO! It's not my time, it's not fair, I'm not ready, this can't be happening to me . . .

Regrets –
I'm sorry . . .
I wish I had . . .
I wish I hadn't . . .
I should have . . .
I shouldn't have . . .
I don't know if I can forgive myself for . . .
I feel guilty that . . .
Why did I spend so much time . . . ?
Why didn't I spend more time . . . ?
Why didn't I . . . ?
I wish I hadn't put off . . .
I wish . . . were here with me

Resentments –
I still haven't forgiven _____ for . . .

84

If it hadn't been for _____, . . . (how things
might have been different)

Things I Wanted to Do Before I Died –
I never got to . . .
I was going to . . .
It would have made a difference if . . .

Undelivered Communications –
I didn't tell _____ . . .
I wonder if _____ forgives me for . . .
_____ never told me . . .

Unfulfilled Expectations/Disappointments –
I thought that by now . . .
I just got started . . .

Realizations –

Things I'm Grateful For –

Things I'm Proud Of –

Things that Made the Most Difference –

85

What I Would Have Done Differently –

What I Can Surrender To –

What I Can Let Go Of –

Poignant Memories (with strong emotions of any kind) –

What Can I Control About How I Die, and What Do I Want?

How I'd Like to be Remembered –

How I'd Like People to Celebrate My Life –

Even without going through the whole process of imagining dying, I often find it useful just to ask myself the questions,

> If I were to realize in the next moment that I'm dying . . . Would it be okay that I'm doing what I'm doing, I am where I am, I'm with whomever

86

I'm with? What regrets, concerns, fears, and
incompletions are there?

Our minds can play tricks on us – can convince us
there's nothing incomplete, no regrets, etc. – I know
mine does. So if I have any doubt about it – especially
if something has occurred between me and a friend or
family member (i.e., someone I care about), I ask
myself,

If *they* were to die before I see them again,
what would I wish I had (or hadn't) said or
done?

These questions help me circumvent my trickster mind
and get to the truth and the actions I need to take in
order to be complete.

What comes up in this exercise contains information
about exactly what to focus on, what to change (if
anything), what to start doing or stop doing in the next
days, weeks, months, or years of our lives.

We can do this exercise whenever we want, and give
ourselves the opportunity to tell the truth about the
life we've been living, and – if we want – the
opportunity to make "mid-course corrections".
Perhaps that's more freeing than living oblivious to our
mortality and having to face it all at once as we're
dying, when we *could* be experiencing that most
important moment consciously and even gratefully.

* *Journaling Questions!* * Imagining Death – an Ancient Practice

If I knew I had six months to live . . .

- Who and how would I be?

- What would I change, quit, start, or finish?

- Whom would I forgive?

- From whom would I ask forgiveness?

- With whom would I spend more time?

- What promises – to myself or others – would I keep, let go of, or remake?

Mining the Gold – Working with What Comes Up

This chapter is an opportunity to work with what came up in the last chapter in greater detail, and to apply some of the practices we've considered, as well as tools and other suggestions that will be presented here.

If you don't feel you need that much guidance to work with what came up, I suggest you read this section on **"What We've Explored So Far"** and then, perhaps, skip to the section entitled **"Forgiveness"** starting on page 103.

What We've Explored So Far

Let's first take a look at what we've covered so far in this book, as we get ready to make use of the information we gathered in "Imaging Death – an Ancient Practice".

What I've intended to communicate about death is the following:

- Many of our fears about death and dying – once they are explored – turn out to be unfounded and/or really about what we're afraid we might not have accomplished or experienced in life.

- Not exploring our fears about death could very well be limiting our experience of living.

89

- Based on the reports of people who've had Near Death Experiences, the process of dying itself might actually be a moving, joyful experience; we can certainly feel confident it will be less painful – emotionally and physically – if we are as ready as we can be and if we don't resist it.

- There is much scientific, as well as spiritual, evidence to suggest that who we really are – energy, soul, a complete fractal or hologram of all that is – doesn't ever disappear, but only changes form. Another way of looking at it is that – in dying – we once again become all that is and re-experience ourselves as vast and unending. Like drops of rain returning to the ocean and melting blissfully into our larger Self, our original home.

- The practices of Taking Ownership, Surrendering, Being Complete, Being Present, and Cultivating Gratitude can help us die with less suffering, as well as help us live with more freedom and happiness along the way.

- Practicing Dying is a common and highly-recommended practice in many religions and spiritual practices, giving us the clues we need to both live and die more fully, consciously, and gratefully.

Working with What Came Up in the Exercise

In many cases, just taking the opportunity to imagine dying and to notice what comes up is a huge step in itself and can have a big effect on your life and your plans. Some of what came up can easily be remedied or addressed; other items will require more attention and work; still others may require help from outside resources. But be assured that there is much you can do on your own to complete the things that came up for you.

We're going to look at the different types of issues and concerns that might have come up, and I'll have some suggestions of how to work with them. But this is your work, so there's no right way to do this except what works for you, what empowers you.

Get creative! Make up personal rituals for forgiving, letting things go, saying "goodbye" to things; taking ownership of the "hard" stuff, the things you'd rather not face; expressing gratitude, anger, fear, sadness, regret, resentment, joy, appreciation. A *ritual* is "a ceremonial act or actions" (Merriam Webster Dictionary); according to Wikipedia.com, "a set of actions, performed mainly for their *symbolic* value".

Some rituals are things we do on a regular basis, like listing what we're grateful for each night as we go to bed. Other rituals might be created for a specific purpose; for example, writing a letter of forgiveness or apology to someone who has died, and then burning that letter in the fireplace, or burying it, or tearing it up and using the pieces as part of a collage representing the future we're creating for ourselves.

Again – there are no rules or right ways to do this . . .
only what is effective and empowering for whoever is
doing it.

As we move into working with the actual material, I'd
like to refer to what's commonly known as "The
Serenity Prayer" (by Reinhold Niebuhr, originally
untitled):

> **God, grant me the serenity to accept the
> things I cannot change,
> The courage to change the things I can,
> And the wisdom to know the difference.**

Again and again as we go through what came up in the
exercise, we can ask ourselves:

- What is the issue?

- Can I do anything about it?

- If yes, what is the first step I will take toward it,
  and by when?

- If not, what can I do to forgive, accept, reframe,
  or transform the issue, my perception of it, or
  my relationship with it?

- What is the first step I will take toward *that*,
  and by when?

I usually find, when I'm working with something that
isn't at first obvious or easy to resolve, that – if I keep
"backing up" from it or "peeling away the layers" (as of
an onion), I can almost always get to something about
it that I can accept or feel some power about.

Sometimes it's too much to tackle something in the form in which it first presents itself to me – I have to peel away and peel away until there's something I can tackle.

For example, let's say I haven't forgiven myself for something I said to my father just before he died, and I realize I'm still not ready to forgive myself. So I "back up" a little: am I willing to forgive myself for not being ready to forgive myself? Hmmm . . . no . . . I think I should be able to forgive myself. Okay, I'll try another approach: am I willing to acknowledge who I am now for being someone who would not say what I said if such a situation presented itself today? Hmmm . . . yes, okay, I'm willing to acknowledge myself for that. And that gets me unstuck and at least started on the road of resolution.

I know that – when we're not in the middle of something like this – this might seem to be an overly-simplistic approach. But when we *are* in the middle of something like this that seems unresolvable, we need some simple ideas and suggestions to lovingly get us moving; we just aren't in a place to accept the "grander" solutions in those moments. And resisting or trying to force things usually makes it seem even more unresolvable and us even less able.

3 Basic Steps

Let's start with a broad view of a basic process you might use for working with what came up:

1. Categorize the Item

2. Identify Next Steps (using different tools/approaches based on the category)

3. Take Action

1. <u>Categorize</u>

As you go through what came up for you, identify each item according to a "category"; for example:

    a. Regrets/Things I'm Sad or Sorry About

    b. Resentments/Things I'm Angry or Resentful About

    c. Things I need/want to complete (with myself)

    d. Things I need/want to complete (with someone else)

    e. Poignant Memories (specific times or relationships with strong emotions attached)

f. Things I'd Love to Do (Dream List or
    Bucket List)

I'm aware of two things with this approach:

-   There will be some overlap – don't worry – this
    doesn't have to be perfect . . . it's for your use
    only.   Do this in whatever way is most
    empowering to you and allows you to address and
    complete as many items as possible.

-   There isn't a "Fears" category. That's because – in
    my experience – the things we are afraid of can
    often be boiled down to one of these other
    categories, which also makes them more concrete
    and actionable.

    For example – if I'm afraid I'll end up in some
    kind of coma for months or years, that could go
    under "Things I need/want to complete (with
    myself): sign an Advanced Health Directive or
    assign a Health Care Proxy" (see "Making Your
    Wishes Known – Legal and Practical Issues").

    Another example – if I'm afraid of the dying
    process, that could go under "Things I need/want
    to complete (with myself and/or others): read
    books on Near Death Experiences; start a group
    to explore death; do some guided visualization to
    prepare myself (and to help me relax about
    changes and losses in general)".

However, we can't always eliminate fear by *doing*
something. Sometimes we have to just practice ways
to be with the fear or the disappointment.

2. Identify Next Steps – Tools that Can Help

a. **What's So?** – Back in the section on the practice of "Surrendering", I introduced a tool called "What's So?". This is a series of 3 questions that helps "unknot" something we're feeling upset or incomplete about, so that we can more clearly see what might need to be done, or at least where to start:

- What is/was the *Undelivered Communication*?

- What is/was the *Thwarted Intention*?

- What is/was the *Unfulfilled Expectation*?

When we're upset (regretful, resentful, angry, sad, etc.) about something, there is almost always a clear answer to at least one of these questions.

b. **Completion Matrix** – As you're examining, categorizing, putting your items through the What's So? process, it will start to become clear what's incomplete and what you need or want to do about them. You may find it useful to draw a simple matrix like I use when I'm doing a Completion Inventory – either in my everyday life, or in conjunction with practicing dying. It can contain the following columns, or entries, for each item to be completed:

Who? – with or about whom do I need to clear something up, communicate, apologize, forgive, write a letter, etc.

What? – what exactly am I going to do?

How? – how will I accomplish that, or what's the first step I'm going to take?

When? – either when or by when will I take that step?

Complete – insert a check mark or the date the action was completed.

Some Examples

1. Item: Burial
   a. Who? Me
   b. What? Complete "Funeral Instructions" form
   c. How? Get witnessed and notarized, copies to children
   d. When? Write draft by 2/1
   e. Complete ____

2. Item: Outstanding Loan
   a. Who? Kathy
   b. What? Propose repayment schedule
   c. How? Call to schedule meeting
   d. When? Call today, meet by end of month
   e. Complete ____

97

3. Item: Apologize
   a. Who? Frank
   b. What? Leaving without saying
      goodbye
   c. How? Write and mail letter
   d. When? By 2/15
   e. Complete ____

As you can see, these examples are pretty straightforward, and this is an appropriate tool for the more straightforward items.

3. Take Action

For many of the items that come up, going through the "What's So?" exercise and the Completion Matrix can clarify what needs to be done and give you a framework for following through with your intentions.

However, other items will not be quite so straightforward; it might not be quickly obvious what actions need to be taken. Some of these are items I would categorize as "Poignant Memories". I believe they deserve their own special treatment, in both Steps 2 and 3 – Identify Next Steps and Take Action.

Poignant Memories

When we imagine dying – and at many other times throughout our lives – we might notice what I call "Poignant Memories" – memories which carry with them strong emotions of any kind. These are full of information for actions we can take . . . if we develop our ability to tap them for that information. Sometimes we just get bogged down with or overwhelmed by the emotions they bring up, so it takes practice to shift into a kind of *observer* or *witness* perspective in order to see what else is there that can inform and empower us.

There are several questions that I feel can help us make the best use of these memories that surface:

1. What was the Person/Relationship, Period of Time, Experience, or Event this memory represents?

2. What emotion(s) are connected with this memory?

   a. (First emotion) what is it about the memory that elicits that emotion in me?

   b. (Second emotion) what is it about the memory that elicits that emotion in me?

   c. etc.

3. What might that tell me? How might I use that information to complete the past and/or positively influence the present and future?

   a. First emotion

   b. Second emotion

   c. etc.

Examples

A. "That first love"

    1. Relationship with H.L.

    2. Emotions

        a. Happiness about the shared love and fun

        b. Sadness that my current relationship isn't as much fun

        c. Anger about being mistreated

    3. What might these emotions tell me, what might I do to experience completion of the past and/or positively influence my future?

        a. Happiness -> Feel gratitude for the love and the fun; remind myself that that's possible for me now

        b. Sadness -> (also) gratitude for what was there; take some steps to increase lovingness and fun in current relationship

        c. Anger -> practice forgiveness; be on the lookout for ways that I "mistreat" or disrespect others

B. Summer Camp

    1. Happy Trails Camp 1970-1978

    2. Emotions

        a. Appreciation for the opportunity provided by grandmother

        b. Nostalgia for being outdoors and working with kids as counselor-in-training

    3. What might these emotions tell me?

        a. Appreciation -> send Grandma thank-you letter; start savings account to send *my* grandchildren to summer camp or donate money to make it possible for other kids

        b. Nostalgia – look into possibility of camp directorship or camp-like weekend activities, volunteering at local Y or Boys/Girls Club

One thing I notice – with these Poignant Memories as well as with any emotions that come up when I imagine dying – is that *sadness* often calls naturally for *gratitude*. I'm sad because I'm missing something – in other words, I appreciated it. Here's where our practice of Cultivating Gratitude can help us focus on how happy we are to have had the experience, rather than how sad we are to no longer have it.

101

The other side of that is that maybe there is something I can do now, in the present, to create a similar experience for myself – an experience that generates similar emotions or satisfies the same needs or intentions as the earlier experience.

And, just as sadness naturally calls for gratitude, so *anger* and *resentment* naturally call for *forgiveness*, which we'll explore more fully, below.

Being present with our own anger and resentment may also call us to be more aware of what *we* do that might hurt or anger others. So observing the emotions and asking ourselves questions about them can teach us a lot about what our heart desires, how we can be more compassionate, happy, and fulfilled, and what we need to do in order to be complete.

And then, of course, there will be many opportunities to practice surrendering and letting go [of attachment]. I want to reiterate that I don't mean pretending something doesn't bother us, but to go fully into the feelings, see what they're telling us, and either take action or let go, as sometimes letting go is the only action to take.

Every once in a while, I notice that I don't seem to want to let go of a hurt, resentment, guilty feelings, nostalgia, sadness – even though I'd call these negative emotions – I just seem to want to hang on to them. How could that be?

Sometimes there is a kind of "juice" or energy – even a deliciousness associated with holding on to such feelings. It may sound silly, and it often is, but our mind usually has some kind of "logic", some reason for holding on, if even it's a kind of twisted or self-defeating logic. I've noticed for myself that – once I can stop criticizing myself for doing such a silly thing, I can start to see what might be operating behind the scenes, so to speak. It might be the logic of a 4-year-old me, especially a hurt or scared 4-year-old me, and from *her* perspective, it might begin to make sense. As I can develop compassion for myself, I can eventually let go of the disempowering feeling or attitude.

Other questions we can ask ourselves about such situations are, *what is the <u>essence</u> of this, of which I don't want to let go? What am I getting from it? Or what am I <u>trying</u> to get from it? How might I get that essence I'm wanting in a more empowering way, in the present?*

Forgiveness

In this framework of "3 Basic Steps", Forgiveness can be a useful *tool* for us to use during Step 2 (Identify Next Steps); it can also be considered an *action* for us to take in Step 3 (Take Action), and it can always be considered a *practice*.

So much has been so eloquently written about forgiveness . . . what stands out about it in my mind is that forgiveness releases the forgiver even more than the forgiven.

If I am holding on to resentment – or to guilt for something I feel I need forgiveness for – regardless of what the other person is feeling, I am the one living

103

with the resentment or the guilt. And since I am the only one who can change my own attitude, and the only one whose attitude I can change, working with myself is the most effective place to start.

> **Forgive others, not because they deserve**
> **forgiveness, but because you deserve peace.**
> *(source unknown)*

In his profound book <u>A Year to Live</u>, Stephen Levine gives himself one year to live *as if it were his last.* His book goes deeply into practices – many based on mindfulness and meditation – that help himself and the reader heal themselves emotionally, psychologically, and spiritually, as they come to terms with their [imagined] approaching death. Forgiveness is, of course, an important part of the journey.

> **Forgiveness renews life by finishing**
> **unfinished business . . . We may insist that**
> **we are not in pain, but that is a measure**
> **of how numb we have become, and how**
> **much we have had to harden the belly to**
> **armor against our grief . . . But death is a**
> **gentle kick in the ass if we can still feel it.**
> **It reminds us to forgive now before it's too**
> **late to say "I forgive you" or free ourselves**
> **from self-recrimination.**
> *Stephen Levine, <u>A Year to Live</u>*

Levine goes on to say that forgiveness is not the same as condoning the act or behavior, but more an act of mercy toward the "actor whose unskillful ways led to such unskillful conduct".

And let's not forget, forgiveness is something we must extend to ourselves as much as to others – that may even be the first place to start.

Is it ever too late?

In my opinion, no, it is never too late to open our hearts, to allow them to soften and be present – even if only to the possibility of forgiveness. This is the goal – the softening, the possibility of unconditional love, for ourselves and others.

Given that we are the ones holding on to resentment and/or guilt, much of the work can be effectively accomplished with ourselves alone in any case. All kinds of rituals, ceremonies, meditations, and creative processes (like making art and writing letters) can fulfill the purpose of identifying and releasing the act, the behavior, and the attachment to the resentment or guilt. We can empower – authorize – ourselves to invent what works for us.

But what if the other person has died or is unavailable or unwilling to communicate? Again – since it is our resentment or guilt that keeps us incomplete, we always have the possibility of forgiveness. That being said, it can be very cathartic to find creative ways of apologizing, or extending forgiveness, to someone who is not physically present.

Is it preferable to forgive or apologize directly to the person involved, while they are still alive? Not always, but often, yes. For many of us, just the act of making ourselves vulnerable – whether we're wanting to release a resentment or ask for forgiveness – is an enormous step in softening our heart, allowing ourselves to experience the pain we might have been avoiding, and feeling the sweet release and relief of letting it go.

Does the other person always accept our apology or do/say what we think they should when we've felt wronged by them?   No.   But – since we can only control ourselves, our actions, our apologies and forgiveness – it's only on ourselves that we need to focus.   Not that we shouldn't be aware of how our communications "land" with the other party . . . just that we can't control how they respond and whether they take responsibility, in the way that we're trying to.

Writing Letters

Many people find that writing letters can be an effective way of completing something with someone – whether it's apologizing, asking forgiveness, communicating your own hurt or disappointment, or expressing gratitude.   It's up to you whether or not you actually send the letters to recipients who are still alive and available.   Often it's powerful enough just to take the time and effort to get in touch with your true feelings and express them completely on paper.   Then you can decide what action to take next – send the letter?   Destroy it or honor it with some kind of ritual?

Rituals

We talked earlier about designing your own rituals –
symbolic acts that help you let go, celebrate, feel
gratitude, or forgive. In the case of a letter you might
write, you could create a kind of ritual by surrounding
yourself with quiet, or with relaxing music, maybe
lighting a candle. You could finish by burning the
letter, burying it in the backyard, ripping it to shreds
or stomping on it, or putting it in a bottle and sending
it out to sea . . . be as silly, serious, dramatic, or
creative as you like. You'll know you're doing it "well"
when you experience a release or relief or a change of
emotion regarding the issue or relationship.

Journal Writing

This is really a variation of letter writing – and of
course the two can be combined. Usually when one
writes in a journal, one knows it's not going to be seen
by anyone else, and that can provide a great sense of
freedom, creativity, and honesty with oneself. When
I'm confused about why something upsets me, for
example, sometimes I just start writing and things
become clear. I can be as silly, young,
"unenlightened", or crazy as I want, which is
sometimes what I need to allow in order to get to the
heart of things.

Communicating Responsibly and Compassionately

Even for those of us who consider ourselves
experienced communicators, it never hurts to remind

ourselves – or to re-learn about – what ways of communicating are kinder and more effective than others.

One tool for communicating that I try to remember is using "I" statements. When I want to communicate to someone else how hurt I feel about something they did, I need to remember to only say how I feel, not what I think they did to me. For one thing, no one can make me feel anything without my allowing it; also – maybe more importantly if I'm committed to having the communication be effective – the other person is less likely to get defensive when I simply share how I feel about something rather than assuming I know what they were or were not trying to do to me.

Another really helpful approach that's relatively simple to learn – although, like any new behavior, requires practice – is **Nonviolent Communication**. Not so much to prevent what we usually think of as violence, but because – mostly unconsciously – we sometimes allow ourselves to communicate in ways that *attack* rather than seek to understand; ways that – again, unconsciously – come only from our own needs and fears, without regard for others'. From the website of the Center for Nonviolent Communication (NVC):

> *NVC also assumes that we all share the same, basic human needs, and that each of our actions are [sic] a strategy to meet one or more of these needs. People who practice NVC have found greater authenticity in their communication, increased understanding, deepening connection and conflict resolution.*

The Dream List (also known as "The Bucket List")

I wanted to give this a different name than the somewhat over-used "The Bucket List", made popular most recently by the film of the same name starring Morgan Freeman and Jack Nicholson. The derivation of the term is from the expression "kicking the bucket", which is a reference to a method of suicide – another reason I'm not in love with the term.

So – maybe the most *fun* result of imagining your death is coming up with a list of things you'd really love to do before you die – your Dream List. Granted, there will be things you'd hoped to do that you now have to acknowledge you're not going to do, and there could be some sadness or disappointment about those. Yep - more opportunities to practice being complete and surrendering!

Here's one way I approach things I realize I'm not going to get to do in this lifetime, for whatever reasons: I identify as many of the qualities, characteristics, or benefits associated with the thing as I can; then I look for other – still feasible – ways to bring those qualities or benefits into my life.

For example, I used to imagine backpacking in the Himalayan Mountains. Now, with neck and back problems, I have to acknowledge I won't be backpacking to Tibet this time around. So, what were the benefits or the qualities I was hoping to derive from the experience, what is the *essence* of what I was imagining? Hiking in nature, fresh mountain air, exposure to a different culture, sparse population, etc. And in what other way(s) might I experience those

109

benefits? Day hiking in Switzerland, France, New Zealand? Taking one of those treks where the indigenous Sherpas do the heavy lifting? When I'm willing to let go of specific pictures of how to get to the essence of the experience, and especially when I'm willing to ask other people to support and brainstorm with me, the possibilities are endless!

You could have some great fun creating or revising your Dream List. Set some specific goals – what steps will you take and by when – to bring your dreams into reality. Get others to dream with you – sometimes doing things together makes them more interesting and/or doable.

This is also a great opportunity to get creative in how you express these goals – put them on a list; go through magazines and tear out pictures to glue onto paper in a collage that captures the essence and keeps it fresh in your mind. Even the least "artistic" among us can make a collage, and it's a wonderful way to engage the right side of our brain and give our overworked left brain a rest.

Working with What Comes Up – The Short Version

1. Identify the emotion(s).

2. Observe and follow them to what they are *calling* for in order to be accepted, resolved, or completed.

110

3. Take action to be complete.

4. Find the nugget of gold – the piece of information or feedback for any shifts or course corrections you could make in your life.

Making Your Wishes Known – Legal and Practical Issues

Some of the fears and concerns that surfaced during the imagination exercise probably had to do with legal and practical end-of-life issues. That's what this chapter addresses, at a fairly general level. Although these suggestions should not be construed literally as legal advice, they reflect, to the best of my knowledge (with assistance from a bona fide attorney in the States of Massachusetts and California) and in general terms, the laws and practices within the United States.

Please note that this information is valid for the U.S.A., and most of the information and forms you need can be found on-line (e.g., nolo.com, legalzoom.com, www.justanswer.com). Residents of other countries may be able to find the analogous information on-line as well.

If, at *any* time in our life, we are incapacitated by disease or injury, we want others to be designated to "handle our affairs" and make health care decisions for us. In addition to writing a Will, designating those we trust to handle matters and make health care decisions is critically important – and it is important to do all of this *before* we are not able to. If planning has not been done – and communicated – our sudden incapacity or death may result in a court's authorizing somebody *we wouldn't have chosen* to make important decisions for us.

These steps – which are relatively easy to take – will ensure that our wishes are carried out and that our loved ones are not left with the heavy burdens of second-guessing our wishes, or of spending months or years and possibly lots of money in legal fees until things are clarified by the judicial system.

Legal Documents

It can be a straightforward, clarifying, and empowering process to prepare and sign a **Health Care Proxy**, **Living Will**, **Durable Power of Attorney**, **Funeral Instructions**, and **Will**. Any lawyer representing individuals will tell you these documents are important for us all – in life and death – and the formalities of signing are easily handled at a lawyer's office, your local bank, or your kitchen table.

Only the **Will** and **Funeral Instructions** are "inactive" while you are alive; the others may be needed at any time and any age. With some thought and intention, you will easily be able to designate people to represent you, talk for you, and act for you if you are debilitated by illness or injury.

Many law offices will prepare these documents for you and charge a modest fee. You may be able to find state-sponsored or Bar Association-sponsored forms on line.

The formalities of signing vary from state to state and for the different forms. These formalities usually have to do with how many witnesses you need for each document (usually 2) and whether or not you need a

113

Notary Public or other type of "official" witness (as defined by the state in which you live).

The privacy of your document is safeguarded – the witness(es) and Notary only attest to your signature *and do not have the right to read what you have prepared.*

Although forms and signature requirements may vary from state to state, the following are quite typical. Each document asks you to answer one basic question:

The **Health Care Proxy** asks: If you are temporarily unable to think or make decisions for yourself, whom do you want to do your thinking and talking and make your health care decisions? (This is sometimes included inside the **Advanced Health Care Directive**.)

The **Living Will** – also sometimes included in the **Advanced Health Care Directive** – asks: If your death is inevitable and imminent, what are your wishes about the use of medical treatment considered "extraordinary" or designed only to prolong life?

The **Durable Power of Attorney** asks: If you are temporarily unable to think or make decisions for yourself, whom do you want to do your thinking and talking for you, have access to your bank accounts, pay your bills, and manage your "affairs"?

The **Will** asks: After your death, how do you want to distribute your personal property, real estate, money/investments, etc., and whom do you want to be in charge of making this happen (the "Executor/Executrix")?

The **Funeral Instructions** asks: After your death, what are your wishes with regard to your body (burial/cremation/donation),   and   what   are   your wishes regarding any funeral or memorial services?

It is especially advisable to name *alternates* for any of the "agents" specified in the above documents.   An alternate is the person you want to take action for you in case the first person you designated is unable, deceased, or unwilling, for example.

As you look into creating these important documents, it is likely you will read or hear about "**Living Trusts**" and "avoiding probate".   What follows is a general discussion of these topics.

Throughout the U.S., there are "Probate" Courts and courts by other names that handle matters involving death and *the transfer of title to property*.   When you hear people talking about "probate", they are talking about the *court process* by which an asset that is "titled" (owned) will pass to the person named in your Will to receive it.

Imagine the following scenario:

- you have money in 2 banks,

- you have an investment account,

- you own a condominium, a car, and an RV, and

- you have a will that leaves everything in equal shares to your 3 adult children.

If you own any – or all – of these assets in your name alone (a lawyer would say you are the "sole owner"), then – at your death – Probate Court is needed *in order to transfer title.*

One way to avoid the expense and delay of Probate Court is to own every asset **jointly** with another. When you are a joint owner and you die, the surviving joint owner owns it all and there is no need for probate.

The potential problem with creating joint ownership is that you give up having sole control of the asset(s), even before you die.

This is where a **Living Trust** comes in. In most states, a Living Trust can establish that *you* are the Trustee (that means you have "legal title" of whatever has been included in the Trust document) *and* you also receive the "beneficial interest". This means you hold the property for your benefit while you are alive, and the Trust document specifies who gets what or who becomes the Trustee of those assets at your death. You have thus avoided the need for Probate Court.

Books and articles are written about this subject. In general, it is advisable to meet with an attorney. Consult the local (county) or state Bar; many have lawyer referral services, and often those lawyers have agreed to offer a free consultation. A good lawyer should be able to explain clearly, in 30 minutes or so, what a Living Trust is and what the pros and cons are.

Communication with your lawyer is critical; be sure to find one who will take the time to help you understand your options.

Related Practical Issues

If the person you assign with **Durable Power of Attorney** is not the same as the **Executor** of your **Will**, the Executor takes over managing your affairs once you have died; optimally, the first will be able to turn things (accounts, etc.) over to the second in an organized fashion.

In addition to the above documents, you will want to put as much information as possible into a **Letter of Instruction** – updating it regularly – so that the people you designate to make your decisions for you are as informed as possible. Not only will this assist you in organizing your affairs and making the necessary determinations, but it will also help ensure your wishes are carried out as smoothly and accurately as possible.

Here are some examples of what you'll want to include in your **Letter of Instruction**:

- List of medications you're taking, your doctors with contact information, and a history of significant health events and care.

- List of all bank accounts: Bank Name, Address, how many accounts (and what type); actual account numbers *if* this list is kept very secure.

- List of all investments and broker contact information

- List of all regular bills, with payee information, how they are paid (i.e., where's the checkbook, or is it done on-line?), and when they are usually due

- List of all debts, with creditor contact information, and when/how payments are usually made

- How to access your e-mail and voicemail accounts (again, if kept secure)

- List of people you'd like someone to contact if you die or are hospitalized, and how to reach them

- List of any personal property (possessions) or real estate that you want distributed in ways other than – or in addition to – what's specified in your Will. For example, your Will may specify that all your possessions go to your children; however, you'd like your 1966 Corvette specifically to go to your best friend (and you can certainly include such things in your actual Will).

For any of the documents and lists we've discussed, it is important to provide copies to the people you have designated to act for you (including alternates), as well as any other close family or friends who might become involved.

Thank You for My Life . . . I am Ready

So. We've talked about why we don't talk about death – our fears, denial, concerns. We've explored several practices that can help us live more consciously and freely, as well as face or greet our death when it comes – Taking Ownership, Surrendering, Being Complete, Being Present, and Cultivating Gratitude.

We've imagined dying, *now,* and worked with what came up when we did that, bringing to bear all the practices we'd looked at and one additional important one: forgiveness, including self-forgiveness as the all-important place from which to start.

In some Native American traditions, people are encouraged to write their own *Dying Song* as a way to be complete with life and to acknowledge the moment-to-moment possibility of death, seen as a *transition* in the great beginning-less and endless cycle of life.

You may have heard the expression in a book or film, "This is a Good Day to Die". Perhaps another way to say this is . . .

> *I am grateful for the life I've had, and I am ready (to live <u>or</u> die).*

What if we could say that and mean it, in every moment? Or notice what jumps up to tell us *"Oh, no, you're not!"* and heed the information and exhortations contained in that feedback to us, allowing it to inform our next steps, shift our course?

For all the fears that cannot be turned into action items, I try to learn to accept those fears, not trying to escape, deny, or fix them, but to be with them and myself with as much compassion and love as possible.

The point is not so much to die with no fear but to live and die as consciously as possible; to do whatever we can to experience life as a blessing, a source of gratitude . . . a true gift.

Margarida's Story – Life is a Gift Freely Given

I've left the story of Margarida's Near-Death Experience for last because I find it so inspiring, and it seems to pull together – in a real life – so much of what I've hoped to communicate here.

In her early 20's, with 2 small children, Margarida was diagnosed with an aggressive, late-stage cancerous tumor in her cervix. Somehow she became curious about and was moved to deeply explore her emotions – what this tumor represented in her "emotional body", and where in her life this emotional situation had originated, which she ultimately uncovered. This was not a mental analysis, but more a following of the trail down which her emotions led her.

At her next exam, the doctors were astounded to discover that the tumor had completely disappeared – no sign of it anywhere – Margarida was completely cured! Somehow she had tapped into a deep

120

subconscious source of wisdom to heal herself. She soon began to realize she could access that source to help others as well.

For many years, Margarida doggedly traveled the world, sought after by celebrities and wealthy people who paid her extremely well to help them heal, with a kind of *driven* passion to help as many people as she could. This was the work that she felt gave her life meaning – what she was meant to do.

But in her 50's, burned out and depressed, she told her boyfriend she was exhausted. Stuck. Done. She wanted to die. That was the only time they talked about this.

A few weeks later, as she was driving back to her home in Malibu from having visited her boyfriend in Northern California, a drunk driver who had passed out with his foot on the accelerator, slammed repeatedly into the back of Margarida's car, pushing her closer and closer to the huge 18-wheel truck in front of her. In order to avoid crashing into the truck, she swerved away suddenly, causing her car to flip over and over until finally landing upside down on the highway.

Slipping in and out of consciousness, Margarida was sure she would die. It was an extreme low place of sadness, as if she had irrevocably lost – or broken – what she now realized was the most precious gift.

Then, suddenly, there was a "higher" understanding – as if she were observing herself from *above* that low place: "everything is okay". She also realized that something or someone had surrounded her, cushioning her body from the hard parts of the car as it flipped.

Because the sunroof was open and she had reached out her hand while the car was flipping, her hand was now wedged between the car and the pavement; the pain caused by the efforts of a couple who had stopped to help and were trying to move the car was excruciating. That was the only pain she was aware of, even though she had broken arms, a broken sternum, and a gash in her head. She lost consciousness.

Margarida came to on a stretcher, her car having been cut apart to free her. Once in the hospital, everyone seemed to be remarking how miraculous it was that she was alive. And she, too, began to wonder why she hadn't died.

She saw that – underneath her compulsion to treat and rescue everyone had been her fear of death; she was trying to somehow save herself from death, or at least save herself from having lived a meaningless life.

Now, as she wondered why she was still alive, she saw that life was being given back to her . . . as a *gift*, rather than a *burden* as she had allowed it to become. A gift, freely given, with no expectations, no requirements . . . no strings attached. "*Being alive* is the meaning; there is no need to *achieve* anything," she tells me.

A page had turned. Margarida's former life was completely gone. She returned to painting, which was her first love, and which she had dropped so many years before. Now, at age 57, she had to look for a job for the first time in her life. Most people would say "there's no way!" but she succeeded in landing a contract position as a Linguistic Consultant at Apple. She continues to know that everything is okay – even when she doesn't have a job at the moment – and that it isn't by *her* efforts alone that she survives . . . thankfully.

Margarida has no more fear of dying, even when she travels on an airplane, which used to terrify her. Whenever she starts to feel that – or any – fear, she just returns to that knowing that everything is okay. And – although there is sometimes a sense of disappointment in having left the (accident) experience where she'd been so thoroughly awash in the sense of well-being – the enormous weight of being responsible for everything has been lifted.

She doesn't feel the need to control anything – in her life or in her death. The only important thing is the experience she is having . . . in . . . this . . . moment. She is completely free.

This is what I wish for all of us: true acceptance and freedom in our lives and in our deaths.

You do not have to be good.
You do not have to walk on your knees
for a hundred miles through the desert,
repenting.
You only have to let the soft animal of your
body
love what it loves.

123

Tell me about despair, yours, and I will tell
you mine.
Meanwhile the world goes on.
Meanwhile the sun and the clear pebbles of
the rain
are moving across the landscapes,
over the prairies and the deep trees,
the mountains and the rivers.
Meanwhile the wild geese, high in the
clean blue air,
are heading home again.
Whoever you are, no matter how lonely,
the world offers itself to your imagination,
calls to you like the wild geese, harsh and
exciting –
over and over announcing your place
in the family of things.

Mary Oliver, "Wild Geese", in <u>Earth Prayers</u>
<u>from Around the World</u>

Appendix A
Bibliography / Recommended Resources

Please note: These Recommended Resources can also be accessed through links on the author's website: www.aboutlifeactually.com

Books

Being with Dying – *Cultivating Compassion and Fearlessness in the Presence of Death*
Joan Halifax

Beyond Fear – *A Toltec Guide to Freedom and Joy; the Teachings of Don Miguel Ruiz*
Mary Carroll Nelson

Breathe to Beat the Blues *(Audio CD)*
Amy Weintraub

Breathing – *the Master Key to Self Healing (Audio CD)*
Andrew Weil, M.D.

Courageous Dreaming – *How Shamans Dream the World into Being*
Alberto Villoldo

the Denial of Death
Ernest Becker

Dying to Be Me: *My Journey from Cancer, to Near Death, to True Healing*
Anita Moorjani

Earth Prayers from Around the World *– 365 Prayers, Poems, and Invocations for Honoring the Earth*
Edited by Elizabeth Roberts and Elias Amidon

Final Gifts *– Understanding the Special Awareness, Needs, and Communications of the Dying*
Maggie Callanan and Patricia Kelley

Graceful Passages *– A Companion for Living and Dying (prose and music)*
Various Contributors, Produced by Michael Stillwater and Gary Malkin

the Last Frontier: *Exploring the Afterlife and Transforming Our Fear of Death*
Julia Assante, PhD and Larry Dossey,M.D.

Life is a Gift *– Inspiration from the Soon Departed*
Bob and Judy Fisher

Life Lessons *– Two Experts on Death and Dying Teach Us About the Mysteries of Life and Living*
Elisabeth Kübler-Ross and David Kessler

Living in Gratitude *– a Journey that will Change Your Life*
Angeles Arrien

Losing a Parent *– Passage to a New Way of Living*
Alexandra Kennedy

Love's Executioner & *Other Tales of Psychotherapy*
Irvin D. Yalom

No Death, No Fear – *Comforting Wisdom for Life*
Thich Nhat Hanh

No Ordinary Time – *The Rise of Spiritual Intelligence*
and Evolutionary Creativity
Jan Phillips

On Death and Dying
Elisabeth Kübler-Ross

the Power of Now – *A Guide to Spiritual Enlightenment*
Eckhart Tolle

Proof of Heaven: *A Neurosurgeon's Journey Into the*
Afterlife
Eben Alexander, M.D.

Reinventing the Body, Resurrecting the Soul
Deepak Chopra

Remember, Be Here Now
Ram Dass

Staring at the Sun – *Overcoming the Terror of Death*
Irvin D. Yalom

the Tibetan Book of Living and Dying
Sogyal Rinpoche

When Things Fall Apart – *Heart Advice for Difficult*
Times
Pema Chödrön

a Year to Live – *How to Live This Year as if It Were Your Last*
Stephen Levine

Courses & Other Experiences – Online, Video, In-Person

Dying Into Love – *"Four Authorities Share What to Do Now To Create The Kind of Death You Want & How To Be of Service to Someone Who is Dying."* (Video)
Dr. Richard Alpert, Ph.D. – aka Ram Dass
Dr. Joan Halifax, Ph.D.
Dr. Dale Borglum, Ph.D.
Bodhi Be
http://www.dyingintolove.com

The Shift Network – *"The Shift Network empowers a global movement of people who are creating an evolutionary shift of consciousness that in turn leads to a more enlightened society, one built on principles of peace, sustainability, health, and prosperity."* (Online, live and recorded)
https://shiftnetwork.infusionsoft.com/go/tsn/wallacea/

Center for Nonviolent Communication – *"Nonviolent Communication (NVC) is based on the principles of nonviolence–the natural state of compassion when no violence is present in the heart. NVC begins by assuming that we are all compassionate by nature and that violent*

128

strategies—whether verbal or physical—are learned behaviors taught and supported by the prevailing culture. NVC also assumes that we all share the same, basic human needs, and that each of our actions are a strategy to meet one or more of these needs. People who practice NVC have found greater authenticity in their communication, increased understanding, deepening connection and conflict resolution."
http://www.cnvc.org/

Conscious Conversations – *"Sperry Andrews hosts several free group consciousness experiences online – every week – in which you can share the truth of who and what we all are with consciousness explorers like yourself. He´s spent thirty years as an experiential scientist, artist, educator and filmmaker directing the Human Connection Institute – so anyone can know what it is like to be 'all that is' with everyone and everything. To find out how this can happen for you, visit:*
http://www.awakeness.com/hangouts*"*

Music

Eight-String Religion, David Darling – beautiful relaxing music by one of the world's most-loved cellists.

Essence, Peter Kater – the entire CD (one long track) – hauntingly beautiful and comforting; I often go to sleep listening to it.

Devi Prayer, Craig Pruess – Track 2 of 3 tracks on the CD, **"108 Sacred Names of Mother Divine"** – this music is mystical, ethereal, and uplifting.

Returning, Jennifer Berezan – the entire CD (one long track): relaxing, grounding, comforting.

Films

Death Makes Life Possible *(Co-Produced by the Institute of Noetic Sciences and The Chopra Foundation) – "This documentary tackles a taboo topic for many in our modern world, and explores a fundamental question: How can understanding death inform how we live our lives?*

"Our guide is Marilyn Schlitz, a cultural anthropologist and scientist who sets out to find answers. Her journey connects viewers to universal questions and also to their own perspectives on the ultimate meaning of life, death, and what lies beyond.

"We meet people with compelling personal stories of near-death and out-of-body experiences, each sharing their sense of hope and possibility about what lies beyond death of the body. Mental health experts help us consider the meaning of death and how we can live without fear, and scientists share how they are seeking evidence for the soul. We also meet people who seem to have come to terms with their own mortality.

"These interviews and the evidence presented by the experts are interwoven with short vignettes of everyday people from different cultures who share their views on

130

death. In "man-on-the-street" interviews, people share their hopes and fears, and we take a look at popular culture images that reveal the ever present fear many have about the nature of their own mortality.

"This film makes the case that we have much to gain by facing our fear of death and asking what death might have to offer our lives. 'Death Makes Life Possible' is a must see for anyone who's going to die."
http://noetic.org/deathmakeslifepossible/home/

This film is scheduled for release in Summer of 2013

_I AM_ – "I AM is an utterly engaging and entertaining non-fiction film that poses two practical and provocative questions: what's wrong with our world, and what can we do to make it better? The filmmaker behind the inquiry is Tom Shadyac, one of Hollywood's leading comedy practitioners and the creative force behind such blockbusters as 'Ace Ventura,' 'Liar Liar,' 'The Nutty Professor,' and 'Bruce Almighty.' However, in I AM, Shadyac steps in front of the camera to recount what happened to him after a cycling accident left him incapacitated, possibly for good. Though he ultimately recovered, he emerged with a new sense of purpose, determined to share his own awakening to his prior life of excess and greed, and to investigate how he as an individual, and we as a race, could improve the way we live and walk in the world."
http://www.iamthedoc.com/thefilm/

The Quantum Activist *– "Be prepared to take a discontinuous leap. There is a revolution going on in science. A genuine paradigm shift. While mainstream science remains materialist, a substantial number of scientists are supporting and developing a paradigm based on the primacy of consciousness.*

"<u>Dr. Amit Goswami, Ph.D</u>, a pioneer of this revolutionary new perspective within science shares with us his vision of the unlimited potential of consciousness as the ground of all being, and how this revelation can actually help us to live better.

"The 'Quantum Activist' tells the story of a man who challenges us to rethink our very notions of existence and reality, with a force and scope not felt since Einstein.

"This film bridges the gap between God and Science. The work of Goswami, with stunning precision and without straying from the rigors of quantum mechanics, reveals the overarching unity inherent in the world's major religions and mystical traditions.

"Meet the man behind the message as Dr. Goswami tells how he moved away from the religious teachings of his childhood, to seek his path in nuclear and theoretical quantum physics, and how he has come full circle, through quantum insight, back to the very religious axioms offered as a youth.

"With a poignant relevance to the problems of our day this film follows Dr. Goswami as he demonstrates how our mistaken views of reality have led to our current environmental, social, economic and spiritual crisis; as well as the means of correcting these errors. At stake is nothing less than our survival upon the planet. The

132

Quantum Activist is a film for our time. It is a film for all time. It is a film whose very subject transcends time.

"Witty, profoundly insightful and colored with humor, the Quantum Activist brings you Amit Goswami's vision of the universe. Steeped in the verifiable facts of Quantum Mechanics, Dr. Goswami dares to pose the question, 'What are you doing to participate in the creation of the reality we all share?'"
http://www.quantumactivist.com/

Appendix B
More Quotes and Writings

"Return to Life"
by *Miguel Angel Ruiz*

I waken
And nothing is the same.
For the first time,
I open my eyes,
These eyes of mine
I long believed could see
And find that all I knew as true
Was nothing but a false dream.

Then, like a radiant star
The Angel of Death
The Angel of Life became
And transformed my dream
From a drama of fear
To a joyful comedy.

So surprised, I ask the Angel,
"Am I dead?"
She replies,
"Yes, for these many years,
Though your heart beat on,
Your mind slept in the grave of illusion
Unconscious of your divinity.

"Now, with heart beating
And body breathing,
Your mind has wakened from hell.
Renewed, your eyes
Admire the beauty awaiting you.

"Your divine awareness wakens
All the love in your being.
Hating and fearing forsaken,
Gone are the guilt and the blame.
Your soul forgives,
Your divinity lives."

My eyes, in fascination,
Stare at the Angel.
Sensing the truth waking in me.
I surrender, willingly,
Without condition.
Humbly receiving
Death and life,
To hell, I release all claim
And with new eyes,
See my eternal love . . . leaving.

from Mary Carroll Nelson's <u>Beyond Fear: The Teachings</u>
<u>of Don Miguel Ruiz</u>

*****

"My Soul Speaks to My Body on Its Deathbed"
by Jan Phillips

It never mattered how you looked
the $65 haircut
the leather boots from Nordstrom's
even the Honda hybrid wasn't that important
What mattered was the night you said
in front of everyone
I'm sorry to that student you'd hurt

It didn't matter that you got standing ovations,
were popular on Facebook and had a few good reviews
What mattered is that you every time you spoke
you told the truth, opened your heart,
dared to cry and laugh out loud.

It didn't matter that you couldn't find an agent,
or a partner, or that handyman you wished for
What mattered is that, as alone as you were,
you kept on working, kept on writing,
kept a comforter handy for the ones needing warmth.

It didn't matter that you let the phone ring,
spent that whole day in bed, took naps
in the daytime to rest your brain
What mattered were those $20 bills you mailed out
to your high school English teacher who lives alone,
those groceries and meals you carried up
to your mother's apartment,
that phone call to your brother offering to come
for the weekend and help him clean out his garage.

It didn't matter that you had a house in the east
and a house in the west,
that you had gorgeous scarves
and jaw-dropping photos on all your walls
What mattered is the dinner parties you had
that brought people together,
made a sacrament of the sound of their words
falling like leaves into the soil of another.

It never mattered that you fell over drunk
from Margaritas, that you traded your body
for a bed off the highway that night you hitchhiked
from Berkeley to Oregon,
that you smoked or snorted whatever you did
before you woke up to a brighter day.
What mattered was that you wrangled conversations
like a rodeo superstar,
transformed lamentations into illuminations,
converted noise and static into sonnets and sonatas.

It didn't matter that you never learned yoga,
didn't exercise like you said you would,
spent whole days in the toyshop of your office
turning nothing into something
that would matter to someone.
It mattered that you had forgiven everyone,
and realized finally there was nothing to forgive.

It matters that you came out,
stood out, spoke out, sang out,
acted out and broke out
before you wore out.

And as you prepare to return to the Mother
it matters now, that your light will go on
to feed the living as your body
feeds the soil where you are laid to rest.

*from No Ordinary Time: the Rise of Spiritual Intelligence
and Evolutionary Creativity by Jan Phillips*
www.janphillips.com

*****

"Letter from Death"
by Lisa Vallejos

Dear Reader,

I come to you in the form of this article simply because
I have found I have no other way to get through to you.
It seems that most times when we meet, our
encounters are quick, superficial and you quickly
push your awareness of me from your mind.

Our relationship wasn't always this way. When you
were a child, you couldn't understand me and so you
thought of fun & interesting ways to grasp me. When
it became too much, you simply put me out of your
mind and went on your way. As a teenager, you
recklessly pursued me as you thought you were
invincible and that your virility would keep me at bay.
Now, your awareness of me is limited to brief
encounters and you cope with me by imagining that
somehow, you are the exception.

138

It saddens me that you ignore me...that you deny my very existence. I have so many wonderful things I want to teach you if you would only stop for a moment and encounter me. People fear me but that is only because they don't know me. Those who have explored me and my lessons have come away much more vibrant and alive... I really want that for you too.

When you avoid me, it's your way to try to deny the passage of time but ignoring the truth doesn't make it any less real. Time is passing...you are getting older...your parents are getting older...your children are getting older and at some point, you will face me. How you live until then is what is really important to me.

You see, when you take the time to know me you will find that I am really much more of a silent partner in your life, inviting you to live. Remember Randy Pausch, author of The Last Lecture? When he realized that he was on his way to meet me, he took the time to make sure that the important things he needed to say were said. He passed on the lessons of his life to his children and became an international sensation as many people pondered how he could be so ALIVE while he was dying. I don't want you to be diagnosed with terminal illness to learn how to live so I'm sending you this invitation in the form of a blog: Meet me and when you do, let me teach you how to live.

To become aware of my presence in your life is the key to living a vibrant life. When you are aware of me, you waste less time on unimportant tasks and spend more time on what really matters. You accomplish the things you've always wanted to but never did. Inviting me into your world injects a certain poignancy, even an urgency to really live life well. It brings the awareness that life is so fleeting and can pass us by in a moment and with that awareness, you can begin to drink deeply of the cup called today. You will learn that you can even face what scares you and come away stronger.

It is now officially fall 2011. It is a perfect reminder that no matter how hard you try to hold it back, time still passes. It is also a good time to ask yourself: how will I choose to live from today on?

We will meet again; hopefully, not before you learned what I want to teach you.

Sincerely,
Death

by GalTime.com Contributor Lisa Vallejos, Inspiring greatness
www.lisavallejos.com

GalTime.com is an online magazine with one simple mission: to empower and entertain women. GalTime is founded on the belief that every article and video we publish should help women lead happier, healthier, more informed lives. GalTime content is derived from a large network of contributors who are a unique combination of highly respected and often award-winning experts in their own fields, and well-established bloggers who have created powerful social and viral networks.

*****

"FEVER"
by Nelly Capra

For days a tight knot
in her arms and chest.
The weight of the world
on her shoulders.
For days, hoping to defeat the stiffness,
she'd walk only
on the sunny side of the street,
stayed away from everything cold.

She did all that and
theorized,
analyzed, examined.
The knot grew tighter
and tighter.

Suddenly she starts shaking
muscles cramped,
trying to squeeze out
all that cold,
like a toxic virus.
The shaking doesn't stop,
there is nothing left to squeeze out
except her breath.

She lies there,
helpless.
Hopeless,
she stops resisting,
she lies there knowing
she will die.

Then the fever breaks,
the tension subsides,
it dissolves into a wave of heat.
She lies there in a pool of heat
delirious, thankful, relieved,
nothing to hold onto,
floating.

*****

"A Song for Dying (Letting Go)"
by Amy Wallace

Breathing In . . . Breathing Out . . .

Breathing In . . . Breathing Out . . .

>I let go of pain, of struggle,
>>trying, wishing, fighting, yearning,
>>>holding on to what it's meaning.

Breathing In . . . Breathing Out . . .

>Regrets and good times drift away.
>>Love, forgiveness – I surrender
>>>all else into Love's embrace.

Breathing In . . . Breathing Out . . .

>I'm me now, endless weightless me . . .
>>grateful to have been here,
>>>ready to be floating free.

Breathing In . . . Breathing Out . . .

Breathing In . . . Breathing Out . . .

142

"IF YOU KNEW"
by Ellen Bass

What if you knew you'd be the last
to touch someone?
If you were taking tickets, for example,
at the theater, tearing them,
giving back the ragged stubs,
you might take care to touch that palm,
brush your fingertips
along the life line's crease.

When a man pulls his wheeled suitcase
too slowly through the airport, when
the car in front of me doesn't signal,
when the clerk at the pharmacy
won't say *Thank you*, I don't remember
they're going to die.

A friend told me she'd been with her aunt.
They'd just had lunch and the waiter,
a young gay man with plum black eyes,
joked as he served the coffee, kissed
her aunt's powdered cheek when they left.
Then they walked half a block and her aunt
dropped dead on the sidewalk.

How close does the dragon's spume
have to come? How wide does the crack
in heaven have to split?
What would people look like
if we could see them as they are,

soaked in honey, stung and swollen,
reckless, pinned against time?

www.ellenbass.com

*****

"On Death"
by Kahlil Gibran

You would know the secret of death.
But how shall you find it unless you seek it in the
    heart of life?
 The owl whose night-bound eyes are blind unto the
    day cannot unveil the mystery of light.
If you would indeed behold the spirit of death, open
    your heart wide unto the body of life.
For life and death are one, even as the river and the
    sea are one.

In the depth of your hopes and desires lies your silent
    knowledge of the beyond;
And like seeds dreaming beneath the snow your heart
    dreams of spring.
Trust the dreams, for in them is hidden the gate to
    eternity.
Your fear of death is but the trembling of the shepherd
    when he stands before the king whose hand is to
    be laid upon him in honour.
Is the shepherd not joyful beneath his trembling, that
    he shall wear the mark of the king?
Yet is he not more mindful of his trembling?

144

For what is it to die but to stand naked in the wind
and to melt into the sun?
And what is it to cease breathing, but to free the
breath from its restless tides, that it may rise and
expand and seek God unencumbered?

Only when you drink from the river of silence shall you
indeed sing.
And when you have reached the mountain top, then
you shall begin to climb.
And when the earth shall claim your limbs, then shall
you truly dance.

From <u>*The Prophet*</u> *by Kahlil Gibran*

♥♥♥♥

Acknowledgments

Sperry Andrews, Karina Fehrmann, and Margarida Moniz for their intimacy in sharing their near-death experiences.

Attorney Samuel Lazarus for his assistance with "Making Your Wishes Known – Legal and Practical Issues".

Nelly Capra, Carole Christian, Karina Fehrmann, Karen Smith, and Derek Joe Tennant for thoughtfully reviewing the many iterations of this book and providing really helpful feedback and suggestions.

Richard Fishman for designing a "must-click" book cover.

Tracy Wiseman for help in developing a pretty cool-looking website.

Francine Lapides, beloved therapist, who has helped me – with great love and competence – make sense of and grow through some dark and difficult times.

Barbara Marx Hubbard and Patricia Ellsberg, with whom I've been learning, exploring, and transforming over the last two years: thank you for sharing and making accessible your visions and your processes of Conscious Evolution and Emergence. My world is hardly recognizable.

Stephen Dinan and The Shift Network – for persisting with your calling, making available the transformative work of so many amazing teachers, for Birth 2012 and beyond. This book is *my* "gift to the shift".

The circle of close women friends who love and support me, inspire and challenge me to keep evolving and breaking free, and are so much fun to hang out with: Carole, Karen, Karina, Kily, Nelly, and Tracy.

The larger circle of friends, family, and acquaintances who have also been supportive and whom I so appreciate having in my life. If you have interacted with me in the last 20 years, you have helped me to write this book. To those of you who have offered your love, support, and coaching along the way – thank you so much.

And Sam, for your sweet love.

♥♥♥♥

About the Author

Amy Wallace has wondered for years why nobody seems to want to talk about death. Seems to her that – since death is something we all have to face, and we never know when – maybe it would be useful to think about it ahead of time, you know, when we're a little more relaxed about it.

Amy grew up in the Boston area and went to college there, but New England just never felt like home. In 1975, at the suggestion of a friend who had moved from the East coast to San Francisco, she packed her belongings into her Ford Pinto and drove across the country. She's lived happily in the San Francisco Bay area during most of the subsequent 35+ years.

Working in the restaurant business and then in sales for many years, she thought she'd found her "calling" in the mid-1990's and started down a path towards a Marriage & Family Therapist License. After earning her Master's degree in Counseling Psychology from the Institute of Transpersonal Psychology (now Sofia University), which is a very cool place to learn and grow, she worked as a therapist intern for almost 3 years before realizing it was not quite the right path. Thank goodness for those sales and transferable counseling skills!

Recently, the idea that having a conversation about death might be one of the most important conversations (ever!) kept tickling at the back of Amy's mind. In fact, it got so tickly that one day - not so long ago - she decided to quit her good solid job in sales to work on this inquiry full-time.

For her, this inquiry - and the book that has come out of it - has turned out to be a happy marriage of her soul's calling and her work and experience in the world of counseling and transpersonal psychology. She is grateful to have the opportunity to engage in something so personally meaningful and fulfilling.

Amy hopes that you find this book about exploring our fears of death meaningful and empowering to you – in living both your life and your death.

♥♥♥♥

Made in United States
North Haven, CT
27 January 2023

31516026R00096